cardio training

cardio training

Keith Littlewood

MQP

About the author

Keith Littlewood spent four years with the Army Air Corps before his career in the fitness industry. He is director of Peak Fitness Personal Training based in London and has been involved in the fitness industry for a decade. He is a corrective exercise coach with the CHEK Institute and certified trainer with the American College of Sports Medicine. He is currently completing his final year of a BSc (Hons) in Applied Sports Science.

Caution

If you suffer from any medical condition or injuries, are pregnant or undertaking an exercise program for the first time, consult your doctor and seek advice from a qualified fitness professional beforehand. This book is meant for guidance only, and if you feel any pain or discomfort while exercising, you should stop immediately.

Picture Credits

p.12: © George, Shelley/SuperStock; p.53: © Bellurget, Jean-Louis/SuperStock; p.88: © Derei, Jean-Michel/SuperStock; p.89: © SuperStock.

This book is dedicated to Beth and Nan.

Published by MQ Publications Limited
12 The Ivories
6–8 Northampton Street
London N1 2HY
Tel: +44 (0)20 7359 2244
Fax: +44 (0)20 7359 1616
Email: mail@mqpublications.com
Website: www.mqpublications.com

EDITOR: Karen Ball
DESIGN CONCEPT: Balley Design Associates
DESIGNER: Jo Hill
PHOTOGRAPHY: Mike Prior
ILLUSTRATION: Oxford Designers and Illustrators

ISBN: 0-681-27887-0

1 3 5 7 9 0 8 6 4 2

Printed in China

contents

foreword

The technological advances of the last century have brought with them a touch-of-a-button lifestyle that encourages inactivity, and this is proving to have a significant impact on people's health. Thanks to this inactivity and our increasing reliance on poor-quality food, there is now a modern epidemic of heart disease, high blood pressure, diabetes, and even heart attacks and strokes.

For many people, participating in exercise is a reactive strategy, one that they adopt when they have had some sort of a health scare. According to the research, people often cite lack of time, lack of motivation, and insufficient knowledge about exercise as their reasons for non-participation in or cessation of a fitness regime. At the same time, there are other people who are following a fitness regime but who are using their exercise time poorly, often doing excessive amounts of inappropriate training or following sometimes anecdotal training programs.

The fact is that a well thought-out exercise plan can do a great deal to combat the hazards of our modern lifestyle. To reap the benefits you don't need to spend hours in the gym and you certainly don't have to do exercises that you don't enjoy (well, apart from a few postural exercises here and there!) If you spend a little time preparing an effective training program, you should find that results can be achieved in a much shorter time-frame.

My main piece of advice to anyone who wants to participate in regular exercise is to find an activity that they enjoy doing. That may be cardiovascular training, strength training, or even a team sport. I hope that this book will serve to explain to people who are new to exercise the major concepts for developing cardiovascular fitness and, for those who want to exercise for performance, will provide a basis for progression.

Keith Littlewood

an overview

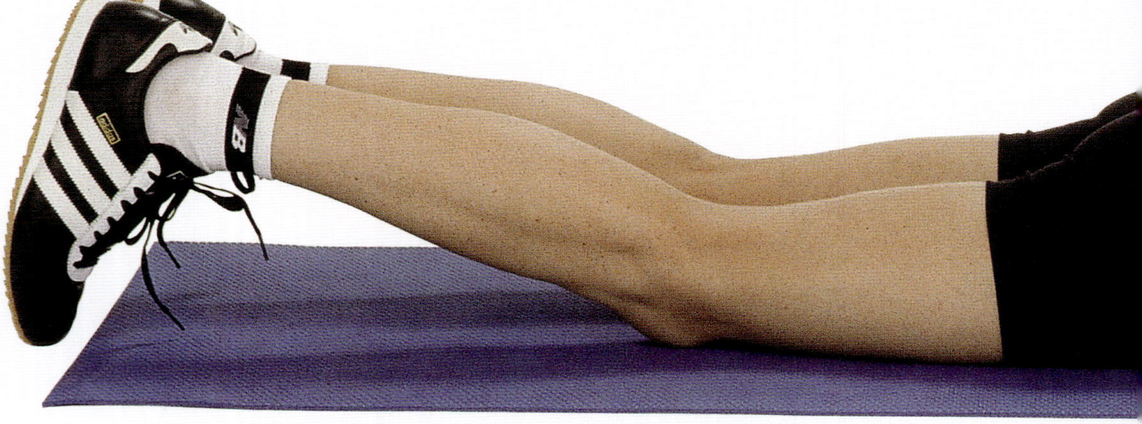

- why do cardiovascular training?
- the psychology of sport and exercise
- the cardio-respiratory system
- the body's energy systems
- the muscular system
- exercise and nutrition
- exercise and aging
- getting motivated
- am I fit enough for cardiovascular training?
- clothing and equipment

why do cardiovascular training?

Training the cardiovascular system to reach optimal levels was a matter of survival for mankind for hundreds of thousands of years. Our existence as a race depended on hunting or being hunted, and for both of these, the cardiovascular system needed to be in tip-top form.

As mankind evolved, the fear of being hunted came less and less from animals and more from other men seeking to make territorial or other claims. One of the first documented instances of cardiovascular exercise was as long ago as 490 B.C. when Phidippides ran the 26 miles (42 kilometers) from the battlefield at Marathon to Athens.

The last thousand years or so have seen a decrease in the need for us to get our food in a physically demanding way, whether by hunting or through agriculture. Thanks to the invention of the computer chip, jobs have become less labor-intensive. We don't have to get out of our chair to change television channels and we don't need to go to the shops for our food—it can be ordered over the internet.

It is no wonder that we are becoming more unhealthy. The statistics speak for themselves: obesity, high blood pressure, depression, metabolic diseases such as diabetes, heart attacks, and strokes—all are on the increase. In fact, cardiovascular disease—disorders of the heart and blood vessels—is one of the biggest challenges to the health systems of the developed world. Increased intake of fat-laden fast foods, smoking, and inactivity promote the onset of cardiovascular disease at a rapid rate. As the body ingests higher levels of fat, cholesterol levels rise in the blood and fat binds to artery walls. The artery walls become entirely lined with cholesterol deposits < which decreases the flexibility of the arteries and so gradually increases the amount of pressure needed to pump blood around the cardiovascular system. As pressure increases, the heart needs to work harder and it becomes overdeveloped on the left side.

Also, since the arteries in the heart and brain are very small, they often become totally blocked. If the arteries of the brain become blocked a stroke will occur, often causing loss of body functions or even death. If it occurs at the heart, the heart tissue will be starved of blood. If you are lucky, you will have a small heart attack that will act as a warning, but more often than not, there will be a massive heart attack that will kill.

The rate of increase in cardiovascular disease has gone up so much that the recommended amount of exercise people are

left > **Eating too much fat-laden fast food, such as hamburgers and french fries, greatly increases the chance of cardiovascular disease and heart attack.**

advised to take has dramatically changed over the last few years. For example, the American College of Sports Medicines (ACSM) used to recommend 3 to 5 sessions of exercise per week, but that recommendation has now risen to 30 minutes exercise on a daily basis.

While some people adopt a proactive approach to exercise and healthy living, others only take up exercise as a reaction to having developed complaints such as high blood pressure, diabetes, and heart attacks. Participating in regular cardiovascular exercise can greatly reduce the risk of developing these diseases. If you are worried about these things, you will be pleased to learn that health and fitness can be developed with relatively little time and effort.

right > **Going for a brisk walk on a regular basis can be very beneficial, reducing the risk of heart disease.**

the benefits of regular cardiovascular exercise are many. It brings:

- improved physical fitness
- decreased cholesterol levels
- decreased resting blood pressure values
- improvements in the heart's ability to pump blood around the body
- improvements in metabolism and in the utilization of excessive body fat stores
- improved respiratory ability
- decreased likelihood of contracting diabetes
- improved psychological wellbeing
- decreased likelihood of a heart attack or stroke
- improved quality of life by improving the ability to carry out daily tasks
- reduction in Body Mass Index.

In other words, exercise is not just for those who participate in sport or performance-based activities. It is for everyone who wants to enjoy these health benefits.

To exercise for maximum benefit, you need to understand some basic things about the body and the mind.

the psychology of sport and exercise

There is large amount of research regarding exercise and the mind and there have been many studies that have shown the positive impact of aerobic exercise on psychological well-being. There are two main theories as to why this happens.

The distraction theory is based on the idea that the exerciser is, at least temporarily, removed from his or her normal environment where high levels of stress can occur, such as the workplace or the home. The other theory is the endorphin hypothesis, which says that during exercise, "feel-good" hormones are released into the blood. The "runner's high" is an example of this. This phenomenon is often accompanied by feelings of ease or lack of difficulty when exercising at moderate to higher intensities.

Conversely exercise, like many other factors in life, can act as a stressor if it is not approached correctly and some people can even find exercise as addictive as any other stimulant. Therefore, you should carefully consider your current stress levels as well as your motivations before beginning a new exercise program. The goal of any exercise regime should be to improve your physical and mental health and to benefit both your body and your mind.

Exercise should serve to alleviate tension and stress. If an exercise program consists of a high intensity workout or extensive time in the gym, you may not experience the stress-relieving benefits that would accompany a more appropriate training program.

the cardio-respiratory system

This is made up of the lungs and their associated airways—the respiratory system—together with the heart and its connecting network of arteries and veins—the cardiovascular system.

the respiratory system

The primary function of the lungs is to draw air/oxygen in through the mouth and its associated airways and into the lungs, and to expel carbon dioxide. The air is warmed in the lungs and passes from there into the bloodstream. This process is called respiration.

Correct breathing, whether you are carrying out your normal activities or doing cardiovascular exercise, involves muscles, too, namely the scalene muscle, the external intercostals, the pectoralis minor and the diaphragm. The diaphragm is responsible for two-thirds of the increase in chest volume during inspiration. If someone's breathing pattern is incorrect, or "inverted," the ratio between the work done by the diaphragm and that of the other muscles changes so that the other muscles become over-developed and you can end up with a forward-head posture that can cause neck and back pain. If this is left unchecked, it can affect the lower back and pelvis too. Before starting cardiovascular exercise you should use the tests on page 74 to help you assess your breathing pattern.

the cardiovascular system

This consists of the heart, blood vessels, and blood. Blood contains a protein called hemoglobin that combines with oxygen to form oxyhemoglobin. This carries the oxygen around the body to the working muscles. As well as carrying oxygen, the blood also carries all the necessary minerals, vitamins, and other chemical compounds such as hormones to the bones as well as to the muscles.

The heart acts as the pump that sends the oxygenated blood around the circulatory system via the arteries and the capillaries, which are the smallest of the blood vessels. Development of the capillaries allows for improved cardiovascular fitness, while cardiovascular training itself actually increases the number of those capillaries.

left > **Exercise systems such as yoga, with its focus on controlled breathing techniques like pranayama, can help you to re-address your breathing and learn to take air more deeply into the lungs.**

the body's energy systems

In order to function, the body, like any machine, requires a source of energy. That energy comes from the fats, carbohydrates, and proteins in our diet, which are converted into adenosine tri-phosphate (ATP) by the oxygen circulating around the body.

If we think of the heart as a pump, then the muscle cells are the engine where that energy generation takes place. At the site of the muscles, an astounding number of complex interactions involving enzymes take place. These interactions act as catalysts to release that energy into the body. ATP is the fuel needed for all the work of the muscles. In fact, the body actually has three energy systems, each of which contributes differently to the production of ATP. They are:

- the phosphagen, PC, or short-term energy system
- the glycolytic or intermediate energy system
- the oxidative or long-term energy system.

comparison of aerobic and anaerobic energy contribution during running		
distance	**aerobic energy system %**	**anaerobic energy system %**
100 or 200 meters	5	95
200 or 400 meters	15	85
800 meters	35	65
1500 meters	55	45
5000 meters	80	20
10,000 meters	90	10
26 miles/42km (marathon)	95	2–5%

the phosphagen, pc, or short-term energy system

This gives short bursts of energy that are quickly depleted. This system does not require oxygen from the cardiovascular system. It is therefore termed "anaerobic" or "without oxygen." There has been a great deal of research into how long phosphagen energy stores last. The exact time depends on each individual but all-out exercise may cause total depletion at between approximately 9 to 14 seconds. This system is therefore the one used to produce energy for sprint- or power-based activities.

the glycolytic, lactic-acid, anaerobic, or intermediate energy system

This gives energy that can last between two and three minutes. It is provided by the breakdown, or "glycolysis" of glucose—derived from the carbohydrates we eat—to form glycogen. The glycogen is stored in the muscles and liver where it is converted to ATP and utilized as and when required. In the glycolitic system, as in the phosphagen system, the production of ATP can occur without oxygen and so is anaerobic. The problem that occurs with the glycolytic system is that glycolysis yields a compound called lactic acid, which raises the pH level in the muscles, restricts the conversion of glucose to ATP, and prevents the muscle fibers from contracting effectively.

left > **Carbohydrates, found in foods such as pasta, rice, and potatoes, are the body's most important fuel.**

the oxidative, aerobic, or long-term energy system

Cardiovascular exercise is accomplished via the most complex of all the energy-providing systems, the oxidative, or "aerobic" system. This uses oxygen as a fuel as well as fats and carbohydrates. The result is that the rate of removal of lactic acid is higher than the rate of production and this is what enables you to carry on exercising for longer.

comparison between the different energy sources

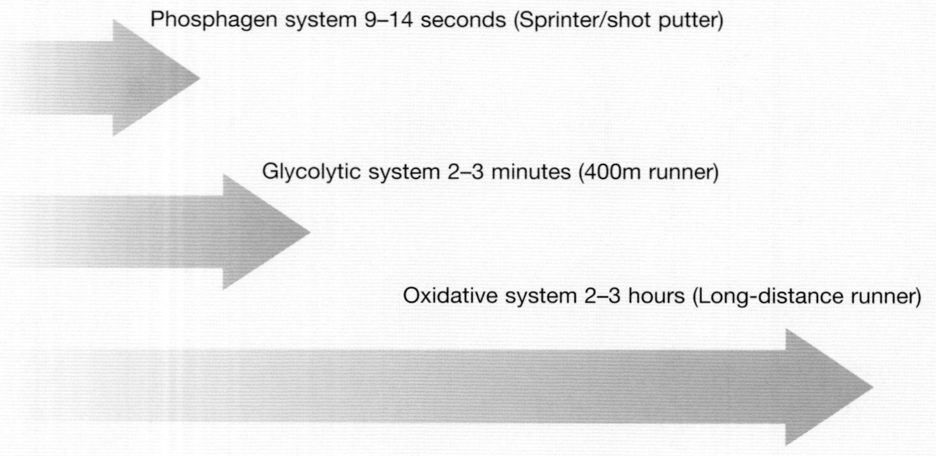

lactic acid—friend or foe?

During lower levels of exercise, energy requirements are met by the cardiovascular system and lactic acid is removed at a steady rate. Any excess lactic acid is taken to the liver and re-synthesized to produce additional glucose for energy production. However, as exercise intensity increases, a shift occurs from the use of fats to an increased reliance on carbohydrates and this results in a restriction of the body's ability to remove lactic acid from the muscle. The result is a rise in blood lactate levels, often termed the lactate threshold. After this point is reached, the pH level in the working tissue will rise, which will limit the cells' ability to synthesize energy and will ultimately cause fatigue. A highly conditioned marathon runner is able to run at or just under the lactate threshold.

advantages of the oxidative/aerobic system

Consider that approximately 60 to 70,000 kilocalories of energy are stored in the body's fat cells, compared to around 2,000 kilocalories in the body's available carbohydrates. When carbohydrates and fats are broken down for fuel, as they are in the oxidative system, they can produce up to 39 and 129 units of ATP respectively. In other words, because the oxidative system uses both fat and carbohydrates to power the cardiovascular system, it can free up vastly more energy than the glycolytic system. The only limiting factor for high energy production is the rate at which oxygen is delivered to the working tissues. Training the cardiovascular system will improve both the rate of oxygen delivery and the rate at which the working muscle can extract it.

the muscular system

The muscular system consists of three different types of muscles: skeletal, smooth, and cardiac, which all have very distinct functions. The skeletal muscles are most commonly thought of as muscle because they allow us to move. This section explains what happens to the muscles when they are exposed to a training program.

The skeletal muscles are attached to the supportive frame of the skeleton by tendons and they give our bodies their shape. Almost all body movement (locomotion) is caused by the contraction of skeletal muscles. They are under voluntary control, which means that we consciously control what they do.

Muscles can be subdivided into tonic and phasic muscles or postural and movement muscles. Some postural muscles are prone to lengthening and weakening. Phasic muscles in contrast are prone to shortening and tightening.

muscle fibers

The muscles in the body are made up of three types of muscle fiber—"slow twitch" (Type I), that contract slowly, and "fast twitch" (Type IIa and Type IIb), that contract quickly. The postural muscles have a higher percentage of slow twitch fibers, whereas the muscles of the upper body have a higher percentage of fast twitch fibers. Sprinters, for example, who do a lot of power and speed training and need to utilize their upper and lower body more than, for example, long-distance runners, develop more of the fast twitch fibers. While the proportion of fiber types in a person's muscles can be the result of a specific training regime, some individuals have a genetic predisposition towards one type of muscles fiber or the other—this can give a certain advantage when they are competing.

phosphagen system	glycolytic system	oxidative system
Fast Twitch Type IIb	Fast Twitch Type IIa	Slow Twitch Type 1

features	fast twitch type IIb	fast twitch type IIa	slow twitch type 1
Contraction speed	Fast	⟷	Slow
Fatigue-resistant	No	⟷	Yes
Energy production	Fast	⟷	Slow
Blood supply	Low	⟷	High

The different energy systems supply energy to the different muscle fibers, as shown in the table at the bottom of page 17. The features of each muscle-fiber type affect performance. Slow twitch fibers are resistant to fatigue thanks to their good blood supply. By improving cardiovascular conditioning, the amount of capillaries supplying fibers with blood can be improved. Type IIa fast twitch muscles are the versatile ones. These muscles

main muscle groups (front of body)

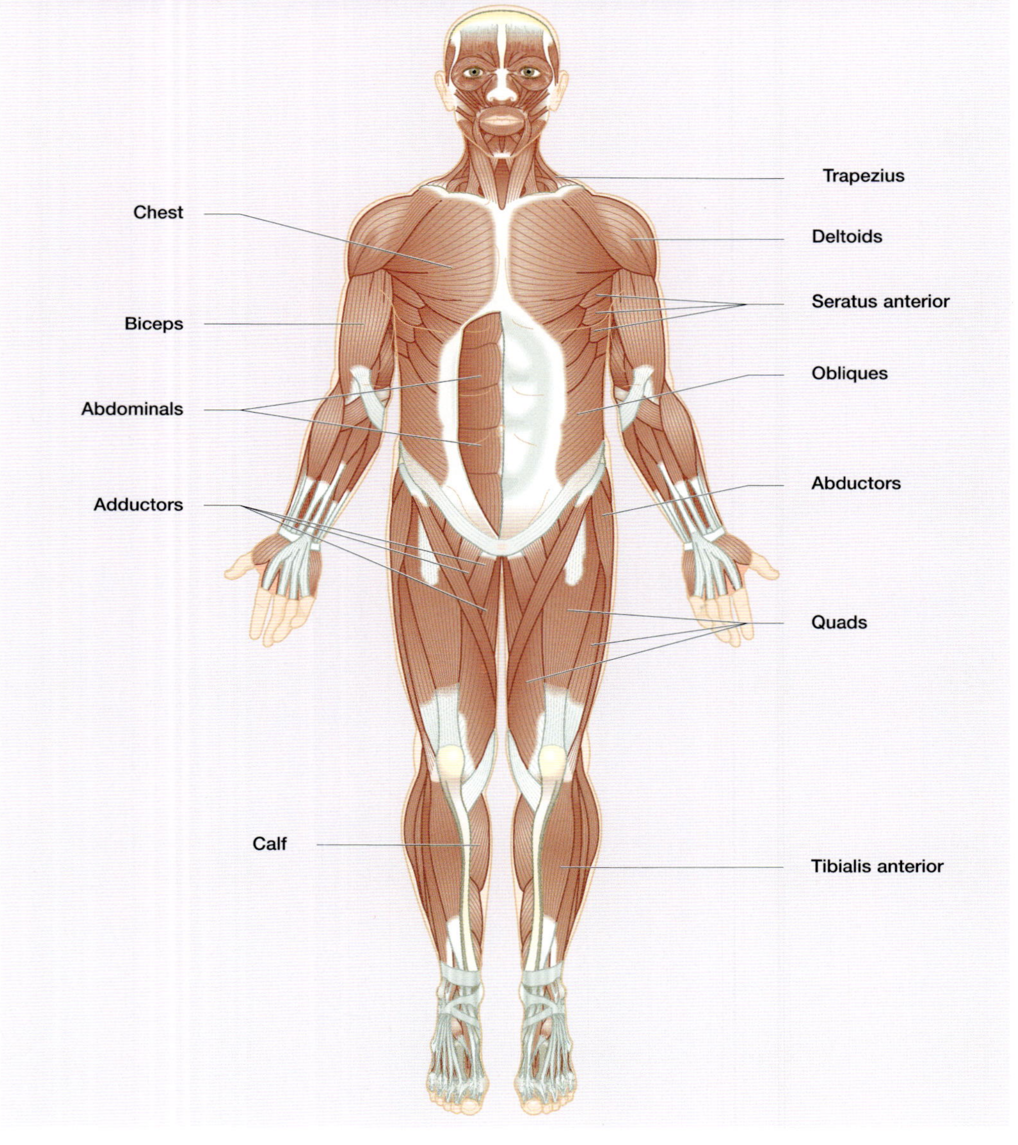

readily adapt according to the type of training that an individual undertakes. If someone participates in an endurance training program, their Type IIa fast twitch fibers will take on slow twitch characteristics, making them fatigue-resistant. Conversely, if an individual undertakes a strength-training or power program, the fibers will adapt to producing energy quickly, just like Type IIb fibers (see the table at the bottom of page 17).

main muscle groups (back of body)

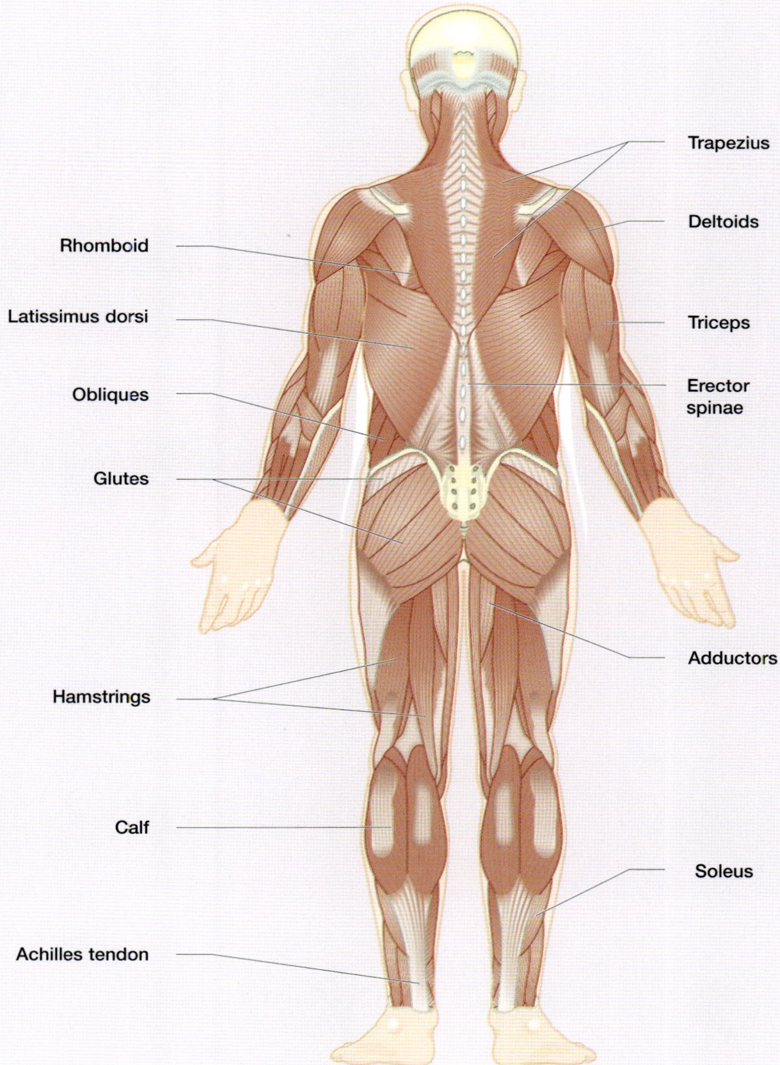

exercise and nutrition

Adequate nutritional intake is of paramount importance, especially if you are following a cardiovascular training program. It is essential for both health and performance.

- Health benefits: maintains healthy body weight, keeps blood pressure within normal ranges, reduces cholesterol levels.

- Performance benefits: ensures appropriate supplies of energy and adequate levels of hydration.

As well as the fats and carbohydrates that are the two main fuels preferred by the body, protein is also essential. 1 gram of fat provides approximately 9 kilocalories, while 1 gram of carbohydrate provides approximately 4 kilocalories, as does 1 gram of protein.

a balanced diet

Carbohydrates are the body's most important fuel. They are the primary energy source for the central nervous system, which comprises the brain, spinal column, and related nerves.

If carbohydrate levels become depleted, protein can be broken down and used to provide energy instead. This results in a reduction in the amount of lean muscle tissue in the body.

There are many different recommendations regarding what a healthy diet should consist of, and the advice can be conflicting and confusing. The traditional "food pyramid" below will help you to construct your own nutritious and well-balanced dietary plan.

In general, you should restrict your consumption of foods that are high in fats, especially saturated fats, since these are often a primary factor in the development of heart disease. Then you should increase firstly your carbohydrate intake and secondly your protein intake.

Diets that restrict calorie intake often heap more misery on the dieter in the long run.

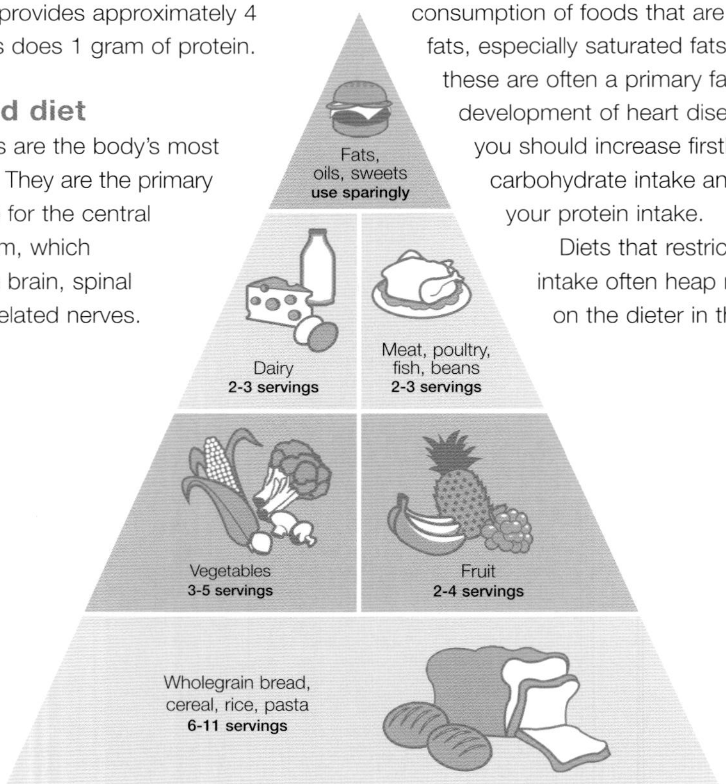

carbohydrate loading—the key to long-distance exercise

The body's carbohydrate stores last for about 20 miles (32 kilometers) of road running. After that, hypoglycemia or low blood-sugar will result. If a person wants to maintain performance over longer distances or periods of time, eating a carbohydrate-rich diet will help to offset low blood-sugar levels and fatigue, and help to maintain exercise intensity.

Carbohydrate-loading, as it is called, should take place two to three days prior to an event or an extensive exercise session, but before that, you should have a high-intensity exercise session in order to increase the amount of carbohydrate stored in the muscle tissue. Athletes may consume as much as 70 percent of their food in the form of carbohydrates during this time. This should be coupled with low-intensity exercise up until the day before the event, as this also assists the body's capacity to store higher levels of carbohydrates in the muscles, blood, and liver.

After exercise, if the goal is to refuel as quickly as possible, you should consume a carbohydrate-rich meal within two hours.

Anyone who tries to lose a large amount of weight in a short period of time will always be prone to regaining that weight. Cutting calories is not the answer. What is needed is a long-term strategy consisting of healthy eating and regular exercise.

the role of vitamins

Vitamins help to regulate energy release at rest and during exercise. There are two types of vitamins: fat-soluble and water-soluble. The fat-soluble vitamins are A, D, E, and K. These are stored in body fat.

Water-soluble vitamins are the B complex and vitamin C. These are not stored so it is important that we get adequate amounts daily. Vitamin C is found in fruits and vegetables such as oranges, kiwis, mangoes, tomatoes, blackcurrants, grapefruits, zucchini, cabbage, cauliflower, green peppers, and potatoes. Vitamin B complex is found in peas, beans, bananas, wheatgerm, pork, eggs, lamb's liver, chicken breasts, almonds, salmon, and herring.

above > **Eggs are nutrient-rich and a great source of vitamins A, B, D, and E.**

the role of minerals

There are eight major minerals used by the body and seven smaller trace elements. One of the most important minerals relating to cardiovascular exercise is iron. A healthy human body can contain up to 3 to 4 grams of iron. This is found as hemoglobin, the oxygen-carrying component of the blood (see page 13). Women in particular are often deficient in iron due to loss of blood from menstruation. Anemia is the term used to describe low levels of iron and one of its symptoms is lethargy or tiredness. If you want to participate in effective cardiovascular training, you should take great care with your iron intake. The recommended daily intake for pre-menopausal women is 15mg and for men 8mg.

Iron is found in liver, steak, mussels, eggs, kidneys, sardines, watercress, apricots, bread, cornflakes (fortified), cocoa powder, chocolate, and curry powder. Many vegetables such as zucchini, lettuce, and cabbage contain very small amounts of iron, too.

the role of water

The body consists of almost 60 percent water and it needs water constantly on a daily basis.

water:

- aids the absorption of oxygen and the excretion of carbon dioxide via the body's cells
- allows the passing of waste products
- promotes the regulation of body temperature
- aids movement by helping to lubricate joints.

During exercise, in particular cardiovascular exercise, there is a significant rise in body temperature and the body responds by sweating, which acts as a cooling mechanism. The amount of sweat produced depends on a number of factors including body size, ambient temperature, and type of exercise. Women generally start to sweat at higher temperatures than men.

- During exercise the body can lose up to 3 pints (1.5 liters) of fluid per hour through sweating.

- Fluid replacement is fundamental to maintaining performance and is second only to oxygen in its importance to life.

below > **Everyone knows drinking plenty of water is essential when exercising, but don't forget it is also important for everyday health, even when not exercising.**

• Feeling thirsty is the first phase of dehydration so you should drink water regularly throughout the day.

• Depending on the physical demands of the exercise you are undertaking, you may have to drink up to 6 pints (3 liters) of water a day.

• A loss of even 2 percent of water will cause a reduction in performance for some people.

nutrition tips for cardiovascular exercise

• There is no need to diet when exercising: just eat good-quality food. Exercise will reduce body fat and develop lean muscle tissue, which expends more energy.

• Eating healthy, organic, nutrient-rich food that is high in vitamins and minerals and free of pesticides will help the processes involved with energy release. If you stick to this there will be no need to supplement your food with multivitamins and minerals.

• Drink adequate amounts of water daily, at least eight glasses, and not tap water.

• During prolonged exercise bouts, ensure that you get 7 to 11 grams of carbohydrate per 100ml of fluid. Check the label before buying a sports drink to use as you exercise.

above > **Ensure you eat a variety of wholesome foods, particularly plenty of fresh fruit and vegetables.**

• Avoid eating 15 to 45 minutes prior to exercise as this may cause low blood-sugar at the start of your exercise session.

low-carb diets—a problem for cardiovascular exercise

There is an inverse relationship between the use of fat and carbohydrate for energy production. When the body is at rest the contribution is approximately equal. During light and prolonged levels of exercise the contribution of the fats can be as much as 60–70 percent. As intensity rises, it is mostly the carbohydrates that provide the energy. That is why "low carb" diets can be a problem for cardiovascular exercise and why a healthy balanced diet is essential.

exercise and aging

Among older adults, there are plenty of veteran athletes who still regularly participate in a wide range of sport and fitness activities. However, the actual amount of exercise needed to maintain physical health and fitness as you age can be relatively low and even a small amount of regular, but effective exercise can be extremely beneficial. The significant difference exercise can make to your quality of life as you age should not be ignored.

An older adult can maintain a healthy heart by committing to an effective exercise program and by taking a sensible approach to nutrition. As we get older, one of the main reasons that our capacity for exercise declines is because of increased stiffness in the arteries, which leads to decreased blood circulation. Regular aerobic endurance exercise helps to reduce this stiffness.

In fact, our bodies go into metabolic decline as early as our mid-twenties and that decline occurs at a rate of 10 percent a year in inactive individuals compared to 5 percent in active individuals. People who lead very sedentary lives or do not take part in regular exercise are those who are most likely to be prone to conditions such as high blood pressure, diabetes, osteoporosis, and depression. They may also lack a range of motion in some or all of their joints. Exercise, therefore, can play a major part in offsetting the effects of aging.

getting motivated

Sometimes it is difficult to get motivated to exercise. You may have started out with the best of intentions and given up along the way for any number of reasons. Perhaps you were not seeing any results physically and became de-motivated, or other activities took precedence and exercising was no longer a priority. Most people have family responsibilities or they work long hours and find it hard to fit exercise into their busy daily routine. After a long and tiring day it can be hard to force yourself to hit the gym. If this is the case, think about the following points:

1 Try to consider what you enjoy about exercise and why you want to do it. What are your real motives?

2 Consider the reasons why you have not hit previous exercise targets before. Has work been the real reason for lack of time or have you had no motivation to bother about exercise?

3 If you are going to start an exercise regime, consider what you are going to have to give up to commit time and effort to it. It may be not socializing one night a week or giving up a couple of hours in front of the television.

4 Try to imagine where you will be six months from now if you decide not to do anything about getting healthier by exercising or modifying your diet.

5 Rate your current motivation level on a scale of 1 to 10. If you choose 5, why 5 rather than 4? If 5, what is it going to take to get you to 6?

6 Now rate your confidence in your ability to stick to a fitness regime on a scale of 1 to 10. Again if you are at 6, why not 5, and what is it going to take to get you to 7?

7 Finally have a good think about what is going to be the real evidence of success for you? Will it be fitting into a smaller dress size, reducing back pain, being able to run to catch a bus, or even running a marathon?

am I fit enough for cardiovascular training?

As a rule anybody may engage in cardiovascular training, whether they exercise for health reasons or to improve their sport or performance-based activities. However, you should go through a simple screening procedure first, to ensure that if you are at a higher risk of having a heart attack or a stroke you are offered the right type of exercise.

The ACSM is the world's leading authority on risk assessment and screening for individuals who wish to follow an exercise regime. The table given here is adapted from their Guidelines for Risk Stratification and is used by health and fitness instructors across the world to assess a person's eligibility to start exercising. It is not meant to replace the expertise of a health and fitness professional, but will indicate your susceptibility to cardiac problems and will indicate if you should visit your G.P. prior to starting an exercise program.

risk factors/positive	defining criteria
Family history	History of heart attack, stroke or sudden death under 55 years of age in father/brother or before 65 in mother/sister
Smoker	Current smoker or has quit in the last six months
High blood pressure	Systolic pressure of 140mm/Hg or above or Diastolic pressure of 90 mm/Hg or above confirmed by measurements on two separate occasions, or taking medication
High cholesterol	Total cholesterol of > 5.2 mmol or HDL < 0.9mmol, or on cholesterol-lowering medication if available LDL > 3.4mmol/L
Diabetes or impaired fasting glucose	Fasting glucose levels of > 6.1mmol/L confirmed on two separate occasions
Obesity	Body Mass Index of > 30 kg/m2 or waist girth above 36 inches (100cm)
Sedentary lifestyle	Persons not participating in a regular exercise program

risk factors/negative	defining criteria
High HDL Cholesterol	> 1.6mmol/L

Count the number of positive risk factors you have ticked and use them to determine your suitability for cardiovascular exercise. If you have ticked the negative risk factor box, this will cancel out any one of the positive risk factors you may have ticked.

low risk—Younger individuals (men below 45, women below 55) who have no signs or symptoms of cardiovascular disease and who do not have more than one risk factor

moderate risk—Older individuals (men of 45 or over, females of 55 or over) or those who have two or more risk factors

high risk—Individuals with one or more signs/symptoms of cardiovascular disease

low risk →	Moderate exercise (40–60% stamina) →	Vigorous exercise > 60% stamina
moderate risk →	Moderate exercise (40–60% stamina) →	Medical examination before progressing
high risk →	Medical examination before starting →	Medical examination before progressing

clothing and equipment

You need appropriate clothing when participating in any type of exercise. Since cardiovascular exercise raises the body's temperature and causes sweating, the best clothes to wear during warm weather or at the gym are a simple T-shirt and shorts. Supplement these with tracksuit trousers and a tracksuit top in colder weather.

Some clothing manufacturers have designed specific climate-adapting clothing that helps to dissipate excess heat by aiding evaporation. This specialist clothing can be found in most sports stores.

Shoe manufacturers have spent a lot of time and money developing specific training shoes for different activities. There is an abundance of shoes on the market ranging from those for the novice to those for the elite athlete. If you are just starting an exercise regime, consider the following points when choosing your footwear.

1 A shoe that is too heavy can affect the efficiency of movement and create dysfunction and pain over a period of time.
2 Top-of-the range shoes are designed for athletes and people who have undergone years of specific conditioning and who have bodies that are accustomed to physical stress.

The ideal shoe for most people is one that is moderate in weight and provides adequate stability. If in doubt, ask a podiatrist or go to a specialist store where the staff are trained to provide information specific to your needs.

When it comes to equipment, there are many specialist stores that sell equipment for all levels. Weights usually take the form of dumbbells or barbells. Dumbbells require more coordination than barbells so you should try barbells first. Ideally, perfect the exercise using bodyweight only, then move on to using weights. Most barbells will weigh at least 13lb (6kg) and dumbbells usually start at 2lb (1kg).

Swiss balls are a simple but highly effective piece of kit to have. The C.H.E.K. (Corrective High-Performance Exercise Kinesiology) institute in California recommends the following size balls according to your height:

18in (45cm) for 5'2" (1.58m) tall and below
22in (55cm) for 5'2"–5'8" (1.58–1.72m) tall
26in (65cm) for 5'8"–6'2" (1.72–1.88m) tall
30in (75cm) for 6'2" (1.88m) tall and above.

chapter 2

fitness or performance?

- training for fitness
- training for performance

training for fitness

For sedentary individuals, the jump from doing no exercise one week to training every day is daunting as well as exhausting. Starting any exercise training regime can seem scary but you don't need to train like a world-class athlete to achieve benefits.

For some de-conditioned people, simply regaining normal cardiovascular function is what they require. Activities such as walking upstairs or carrying bags of shopping without undue distress should be their goals.

Whatever level of fitness you are trying to achieve though, you need to start by learning how to take your pulse, which will give you your heart rate. You can either take this manually or by using a heart-rate monitor. To obtain your resting heart rate reading (RHR), stay seated as you measure your pulse.

a

manual palpation

To obtain a manual reading you need to locate your pulse. Always remember to use your index finger and forefinger to do this. If you try to do it with your thumb you may get a false reading as there is a pulse in your thumb. The three best places to find the pulse are the carotid artery, the brachial artery, and the radial artery.

To locate the carotid artery, place two fingers on the neck directly underneath the chin. Feeling the windpipe, trace around it until it disappears into the neck. This where you should take the pulse (a).

When you flex your elbow joint you will notice a crease at the place where the upper arm meets the forearm. When you extend or straighten your arm you should be able to see the brachial artery as it comes out from the bicep muscle of the upper arm. As the arm approaches its fully straightened position you will be able to feel the brachial artery and can then take the pulse (b).

With the palm facing upward, place both fingers on the tip of the thumb. Now trace down the bone of the thumb until it drops down onto the wrist. This is the radial artery (c).

Once you have located the pulse, you can either count the pulse rate using a stopwatch for one minute, or take the pulse for 15 seconds then multiply the result by four. The result is expressed in beats per minute (bpm). Be aware that this method only gives an approximate rate.

using a heart-rate monitor

These monitors range in price from moderate to fairly expensive, depending on make and model. They make finding your heart rate a simple task and provide immediate feedback on the quality of work you are doing. Most cardiovascular equipment in a gym is fitted with a heart-rate monitor but it can be useful to purchase your own watch-type monitor so that you can check your heart rate when exercising outdoors. Follow the manufacturer's instructions carefully as incorrect use can give a false reading.

c

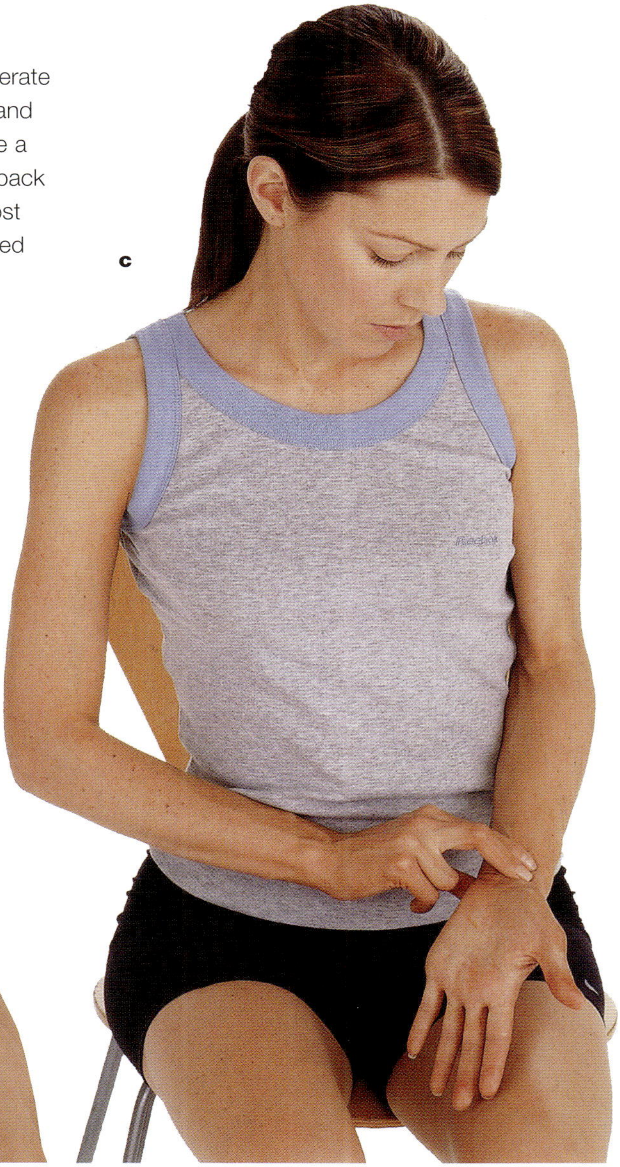

b

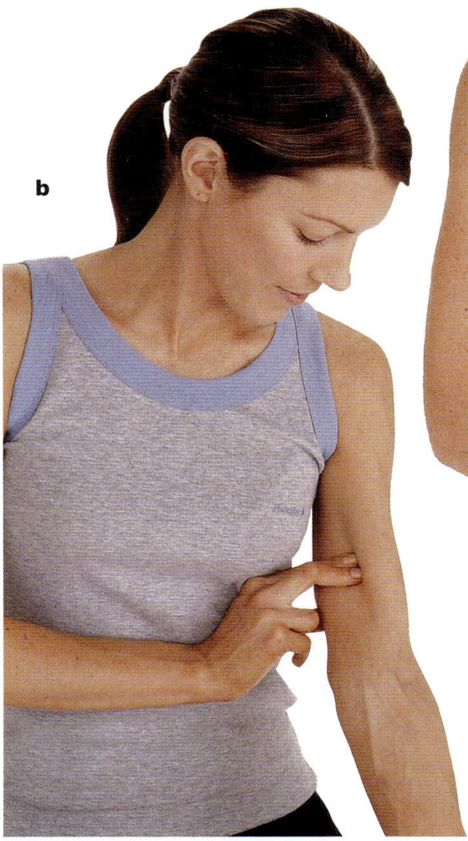

d

On men, the monitor should be placed on the ribcage, just below the nipples. For women it should sit comfortably under the bra strap (d).

As you can see from the table below, the lower the heart rate, the fitter you are. At the peak of his performance, British athlete and Olympic Champion Sebastian Coe had a resting heart rate of approximately 30 bpm.

finding your heart-rate training zone

When you are just starting out, you need to find and work within your heart-rate training zone. This is an age-based percentage of your maximum heart rate, or Heart Rate Max (MHR), and is expressed in beats per minute (bpm). For beginners, the percentage to work at is approximately 55–75%.

To find your Heart Rate Max, you should use the following calculation:

Heart Rate Max = 220 minus your age

To find your heart-rate training zone, simply multiply your Heart Rate Max by your desired range of maximum stamina. As I have already stated, for a beginner that is 55–75%.

For example, for a thirty-year-old:

Heart Rate Max : 220 – 30 = 190 bpm
55% MHR = 190 x 0.55 = 105 bpm
75% MHR = 190 x 0.75 = 143 bpm

This means that as this person exercises, his or her heart rate should be between 105 and 143 beats per minute.

If you wear a heart-rate monitor as you exercise, check your heart rate occasionally to see how you are doing. Alternatively, measure your resting heart rate (RHR) and compare it with your heart rate immediately after exercise.

If you have ever been to a gym, you will have seen a heart-rate chart on the console of most of the cardiovascular equipment. The chart opposite is an example of heart-rate training zones for people according to their age. As you can see, this chart includes a variety of different training zones.

resting heart rate values

rating	beats per minute
poor	80–90 bpm
average	70–80 bpm
good	60–70 bpm
elite	50–60 bpm or below

heart-rate training zones

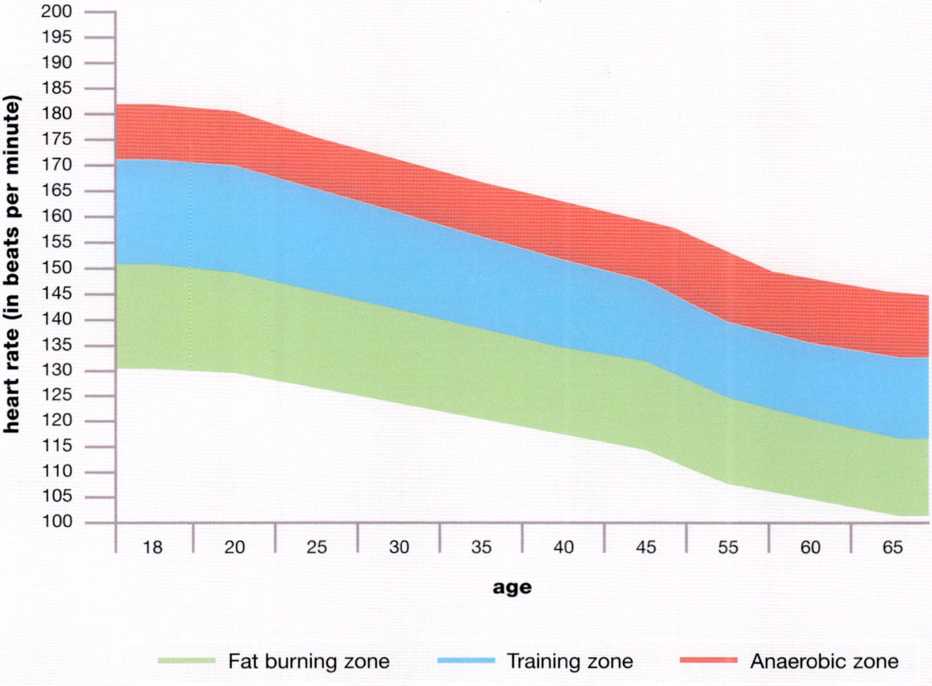

fat-burning zone

This is a low- to moderate-intensity heart-rate zone that keeps the exerciser utilizing fat as the predominant fuel. If you exercise in this zone, especially if you are new to exercise, you will develop your endurance. As you increase the intensity of your exercise, there will be a gradual shift from the use of fat for the production of energy to the use of carbohydrates (see pages 14-16). This is necessary to bring about further gains.

cardiovascular training zone

Exercising in this zone sets in train the development of more capillaries and fat-utilizing cells in the body, and so improves oxygen delivery and extraction.

anaerobic zone

The anaerobic or lactate training zone is important for developing running endurance. It allows the athlete to run for longer periods at increased intensities when applied correctly into a training regime. The result is a lower rate of lactic acid production at higher intensities.

training for performance

If you are training for performance, or simply want to train to a higher level, you need to be able to measure your stamina, or cardiovascular capacity, in order to see how hard you are working. Stamina is defined as an individual's ability to transport oxygen from the lungs to the working tissue during a bout of exercise.

Stamina is expressed as the amount of oxygen in milliliters per kilogram of body weight per minute. The term "VO2 max" is often used to express stamina, but for the sake of simplicity, I shall refer to it in this book simply as "stamina." The measurement of stamina is based on a person's Heart Rate Reserve (HRR)—the difference between their resting heart rate (RHR) and their maximum heart rate (MHR). It is, therefore, a very personal measurement and if you use it as the basis of your training, it will provide you with a much more individual training approach.

The ACSM recommends three phases for exercise programming at performance level:

1 Initial Conditioning Phase
2 Improvement Phase
3 Maintenance Phase.

The Initial Conditioning Phase is designed to increase heart rate, blood pressure, and respiratory rates in a gradual, safe, but effective way.

This phase ensures that Delayed Onset Muscle Soreness (DOMS) is kept to a minimum and that injury is avoided. It also helps you to adapt psychologically to exercise, which in turn helps motivate you and keeps you motivated.

In the Initial Conditioning Phase, some benefits can be seen from as little as 10 minutes per session. Provided that you maintain the exercise continuously and at the correct intensity, 10 minutes is actually the ideal length of time for the sedentary person who has not exercised for quite some time to begin exercising.

	number of sessions	intensity	length of time per session
initial phase Weeks 1–6	2–4	40–60% stamina	10–25 minutes
improvement phase Weeks 7–13	3–4	60–85% stamina	25–45 minutes
maintenance phase Weeks 14–21	3–5	70–85% stamina	45–60 minutes

male versus female

When it comes to stamina, there is a very significant difference between males and females, the main factor being the size difference between the sexes and the amount of lean muscle tissue each possesses. Females have higher levels of adipose, or fat tissue, while males have higher levels of denser lean muscle tissue. Since stamina is expressed per kilogram of body weight, someone with a higher density of muscular tissue will have greater stamina. However, cardiovascular training can result in gains of up to 40 percent.

The Initial Conditioning Phase will vary according to the individual. The following guidelines are an example of an appropriate rate of progression for an apparently healthy sedentary individual.

How quickly you can progress to the other phases will depend on your:

- ability to carry out daily tasks
- age
- medical/risk status (see risk factors table on pages 26-27)
- individual needs and goals
- level of motivation.

The Improvement Phase aims to increase the training stimulus or intensity of exercise. The target for this phase of cardiovascular conditioning is to progress up to 85 percent of stamina, which is considered a vigorous level of exercise.

As I have already said, the level of progress for each individual will vary and it is important to stick to the correct level and not to progress too fast even though you may feel that you can. Attempting to do too much too soon is a common mistake. That is why you should also avoid training with people who are at a more advanced level. When you find you can't keep up, you are more likely to stop altogether. Be patient. The opportunity to train for longer and harder periods is just around the corner.

using heart rate reserve for an individual approach to training

Using a measurement of stamina based on your Heart Rate Reserve (HRR) gives a more personalized approached to your training.

First you need to find your Heart Rate Reserve (HRR). Assume a 30 year-old subject with a RHR of 70bpm, which gives a Heart Rate Max of 190, as already explained above.

Now, HRR = Heart Rate Max – RHR
190 – 70 = 120bpm

Now multiply this figure by the recommended percentage and then add the RHR. This will show you the heart rate training zone you should be working in.

For example, for 40%, the calculation is as follows:

HRR x 40% + 70
= 120 x 40% + 70
=118bpm

For 50%:

HRR x 50% + 70
= 120 x 50% + 70
= 130bpm

chapter 3

how do I train?

- the basics of training
- periodization for exercise planning
- optimal training
- athletic cardiovascular training
- testing your cardiovascular capacity

the basics of training

Getting the basic principles of training right is often overlooked by people starting a new training regime and even those who regularly participate in sport. If you want to learn to drive correctly you need to know how the car works! Taking a little time to understand the principles of training helps you to fine tune your training program and ultimately your body.

No matter whether you are training for fitness or performance, you need to train according to the following principles:

- frequency
- intensity
- volume/duration/time
- type/mode
- overload
- progression
- reversibility
- specificity
- individuality.

frequency

The frequency of training determines how well the body recovers and adapts to the exercise. It is the factor that is most often overlooked by both exercisers and trainers. Most people are stuck in the mindset that says that the body adapts itself to exercise during the actual exercise session. However it is during the rest periods between sessions that the gains are made. These are essential to develop "supercompensation"—physiological and psychological adaptation to training.

For example, when we do cardiovascular training we deplete our energy stores via the aerobic system but between sessions, given enough time—usually within 10 hours—the body is able to replenish those stores and increase them to above their normal levels. This means that the exerciser can then train at an increased level of intensity and performance. According to ACSM guidelines, you should exercise for 30 minutes on most days. (However, if you are doing strength-training there is a higher level of stress placed on the central nervous system and this can take up to 7 times longer to recover.)

intensity

Intensity of exercise is one of the most important factors for enhancing the performance of the aerobic system. It is in inverse proportion to the volume of exercise or to the time spent exercising. For example, a long-distance runner is able to run for long distances at a moderate intensity, whereas a sprinter can operate at a high intensity for a short space of time. You should work to reach an intensity threshold and after that should attempt to go beyond that threshold. However, too much intensity may lead to over-training (see opposite). Intensity may be expressed in many ways:

1 Heart rate—beats per minute (bpm)
2 Speed—miles per hour/kilometers per hour
3 Kilocalories per minute or per hour
4 Percentage of VO2 max or stamina.

volume/duration/time

The volume (amount of work completed) or duration of training sessions is as important a variable as intensity, especially when it comes to developing aerobic endurance. The idea is to increase gradually the amount of time spent exercising. During the initial conditioning phase a lot of time must be devoted to volume of exercise to prepare for the increased demands that lie ahead. High volume low-intensity work during this phase prepares the exerciser both physiologically and psychologically.

type/mode

This is the type of exercise that you engage in, for example, cycling or running, resistance training or cardiovascular training, and so on.

overload

If you never get beyond the thresholds you reach in relation to either frequency, intensity, time, or type (FITT) of exercise there will not be any improvement in your performance. This often leads to stagnation and is a common reason why people stop training. To avoid this, you should regularly assess whether or not you are progressing.

- **Frequency**—how many runs have you done in the session (single, multiple, distances, sprints, or jogs)?

- **Intensity**—how fast have you run?

- **Time**—how long have you taken to complete the runs?

- **Type**—what type of exercise have you done, for example, resistance, assisted aerobic, or anaerobic?

over-training

This is an increase in training intensity and/or volume without sufficient recovery and rest time. More than one session a day constitutes over-training even for athletes. Training excessively means that there are lower levels of fuel available for the working muscles, which leads to fatigue. Remember, when training intensity increases, volume must decrease. In addition, you should eat a good diet to ensure that your fuel reserves are topped up ready for the next session.

The following symptoms have been observed in over-trained individuals:

- muscle tenderness
- decrease in performance
- decreased sleep time
- nausea
- weight loss
- high resting heart rate (tachycardia)
- high blood pressure
- lowered immune system, leading to colds and other viruses.

People who become negatively addicted to exercise often experience the symptoms of over-training. You may be at risk if:

- you schedule your exercise at the same time and do multiple sessions every day
- you suffer mood changes if you are unable to exercise
- you give priority to exercise over other activities
- due to injury, you are unable to exercise and become severely depressed.

progression

This relates to how you "load" your energy systems (see pages 14–15) in order to bring about a training response, or improve your performance. Most people tend to use a standard loading technique, which means that they work at the same intensity all the time. This may be effective in the initial conditioning phase, but in the later phases, you need to use "step loading," in other words, sometimes doing more repetitions (reps) with a lighter load and sometimes fewer reps with a heavier load.

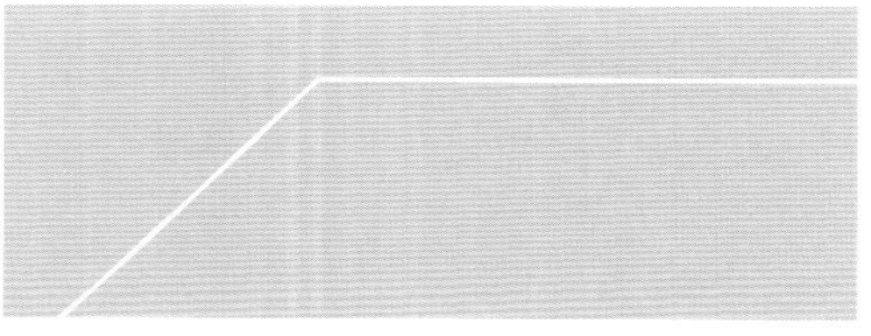

standard loading

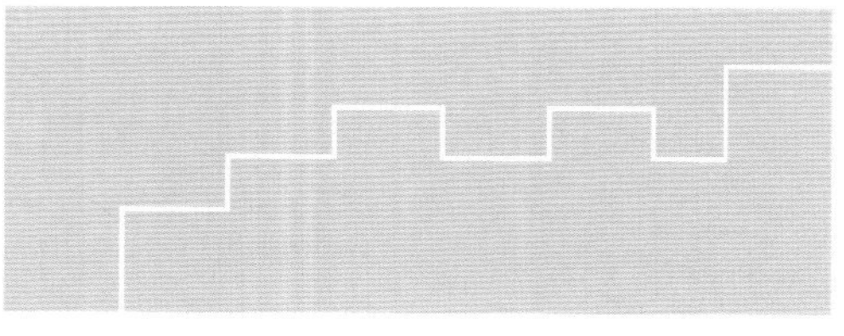

step loading

reversibility or detraining

Research has found that when people stop exercising, their performance decreases within the space of 1 to 2 weeks. Stopping for 2 to 3 months can see a total reversal of the gains made from even a lengthy training schedule. In cardiovascular detraining, the energy-producing cells that utilize fat decrease in number as do the capillaries supplying oxygenated blood to the working muscle. In other words, use it or lose it! Even trained athletes who don't train for 2 to 6 weeks have to go through a reconditioning phase to gradually bring their performance levels up to their previous standard.

People who train for general fitness often make the mistake of trying to train at the level that they trained at before, say, going on holiday. The effect can be demoralizing. Firstly, the body cannot physiologically deal with such intensity and the result will be intense muscle soreness. Secondly, you will feel demoralized at not being able to work as before. The result—falling off the exercise wagon!

specificity

This is important when engaging in multiple activities or cross-training. The essence is—you get what you train for! For example a well-conditioned runner who has a highly trained cardiovascular system will not be able to cycle at a similar level. The dynamics of running are completely different to those of cycling. Additionally, training for strength and cardiovascular fitness concurrently may not be the most beneficial way of training. There will be a general conditioning effect on the cardiovascular system but it will not have a significant impact across all types of exercise.

individuality

No matter how solid an exercise program might be, no two individuals will benefit from it in exactly the same way, physiologically or psychologically. What works for one person won't necessarily work for the next. Individual differences may often occur because of:

- age
- experience
- exercise capacity
- health status
- training load
- recovery ability
- body shape.

periodization for exercise planning

Periodization is the structuring of training sessions into planned segments of a certain amount and intensity. Athletes use it in order to compete at the top level.

Many people think there is no place for periodization in the health and fitness industry, particularly when exercisers' attendance is poor, but anyone who participates in cardiovascular or strength-training programs of three or more sessions a week should contemplate using periodization because it helps you to:

- maintain and improve motivation
- maintain and improve fitness
- avoid injuries
- avoid stagnation
- adhere to regular exercise.

If you want to train regularly you need to have an effective goal-setting strategy covering, for example, short-term goals over a week or a month and long-term goals over the year. You can use periodization to plan your exercise sessions and provide yourself with changing levels of intensity and quantity. Your planning should include times when you might be going away on holiday or for work. You can plan these in as rest or transition periods.

Athletes usually concentrate on a General Conditioning Phase, a Pre-Competition Phase, a Competition Phase, and a Transition Phase, as in the example here.

example of an annual plan

january	february	march	april	may	june
For performance General Conditioning Phase		Pre-Competition Phase		Competition Phase	Transition Phase
For fitness Aerobic conditioning phase/circuits		General strength		Reprogram general strength	Holiday
july	**august**	**september**	**october**	**november**	**december**
For performance General Conditioning Phase		Pre-Competition Phase		Competition Phase	Transition Phase
For fitness Aerobic conditioning phase/circuits		General strength		Reprogram general strength	Holiday

optimal training

When beginning any cardiovascular activity, remember we are all unique in our responses to exercise. Individual stress and fitness levels can affect how our bodies react to various forms of exercise, and training programs need to be personalized to produce optimal results.

Far too many people spend far too long training incorrectly. Taking a short amount of time to understand the principles of training allows the exerciser to develop his or her own specific exercise regimes. This not only optimizes the time spent training but also decreases the overall time needed for exercise.

Activities such as walking, running, cycling, rollerblading, and swimming are limited by levels of fatigue. Success in these endurance-based sports requires a combination of high levels of stamina, well-developed respiratory and cardiovascular systems, and sheer determination. It depends on the condition of the cardiovascular system, its ability to deliver oxygen to the working tissue, and the ability of the tissue to utilize that oxygen to convert body fat into energy. For this reason, cardiovascular conditioning must be the focus of training for the endurance athlete.

athletic cardiovascular training

Athletic training of the cardiovascular system can take a variety of forms and non-athletes can incorporate various elements of the following different training methods into their own personal fitness regimes. However, care should be taken when progressing from low to high intensities if you are new to exercise.

continuous or uniform training

This is any type of exercise at low to moderate intensity over a long period of time. This type of exercise is important in the initial conditioning phase as it helps to develop the cardiovascular system, generates capillaries, and ensures increased oxygen concentration and extraction. It also helps prevent injuries and, as you gradually increase the amount of exercise, it helps the individual to judge their own progress and develop a positive outlook. When you are doing this sort of training, you may start with as little as 10 minutes' exercise, building up to 60 minutes or so as you gain in experience and fitness.

Continuous training is great during the initial stages of endurance training, but it is insufficient for maximal endurance performance. For this you need to incorporate anaerobic or interval-based training in your program.

model or repetition training

This is based on a mixture of continuous training and interval training and helps to prepare you for race conditions. For example, in a 3 mile (5km) race the components of the race are a) fast start; b) the steady bulk of the run; and c) strong finish. If you wanted to improve the start and finish of the run, you would concentrate on interval training to increase the lactate threshold, while if you wanted to improve the main part of the run, you would choose low to moderate intensity continuous training.

interval training

This type of training helps to increase the intensity of any cardiovascular exercise you decide to undertake. It involves high-intensity training sessions carried out over shorter periods of time. During such sessions the lactate threshold increases (see page 16) so you suffer less fatigue. This type of fitness training also increases the amount of muscle enzyme available to help with the production of energy, plus it ensures that even after your training session is complete, you continue to benefit because the body continues to use fats and carbohydrates and so more energy is released.

fartlek training

This is a variation of continuous or uniform training. It helps to alleviate the boredom that some people find sets in during long, moderately paced exercise. The idea is to manipulate the intensity of the exercise by using markers such as lamp posts or trees between which you run, walk, cycle, and so on. Using such markers enables you to modify the speed of your exercise, switching from high to moderate to low intensity in whatever order you choose as you reach each marker. Remember that variety of exercise is the key to staying motivated!

testing your cardiovascular capacity

Testing your cardiovascular capacity from time to time provides you with information about your current level of cardiovascular fitness, or stamina. It is a useful tool to see how you are improving. You can test yourself using the following "maximal" tests, so called because exercisers are required to push themselves to their maximal capacity.

Maximal tests can be very demanding, even for fit and experienced athletes, and I do not recommend them for people who are very new to exercise. Instead, it is far more advisable to assess your level of fitness once you have completed an initial conditioning phase to avoid overstretching yourself or causing injury.

the 1 mile (1.6km) walk test

The purpose of this test is to walk a mile in the fastest time possible. At the end, your heart rate and time to complete the mile are noted and compared against the chart opposite, which shows your units of stamina.

1 First use the ACSM Risk Stratification Table (see page 26) to ensure that you are fit.

2 Do a warm up consisting of light mobilization and stretching.

3 Use a stopwatch to record the time taken to walk (no running allowed) the mile (1.6km).

4 As soon as the mile (1.6km) is finished, record your heart rate over a 10-second period.

5 Using the chart opposite, compare the time taken to complete the mile (1.6km) with your 10-second heart rate to give an indication of your stamina. For example, if a 25-year-old man completes the mile (1.6km) in 12 minutes and his heart rate is 130, his cardiovascular capacity, or level of stamina, is 56.9. As you progress with your cardiovascular training, repeat this test from time to time to see what improvement you are making.

mixing your exercise

Many people who participate in training sessions often engage in multiple types of activity that includes both strength training and cardiovascular exercise. But training between these two modes concurrently may not be the most effective strategy and the result may be that one is developed at the expense of the other. I recommend that people who want to train both these fitness components should ideally complete strength training on one day and cardiovascular training the next. For those who are not particularly concerned about specific training effects, I recommend that the cardiovascular element of training be conducted after strength training. There is little point trying to do complex strength training exercises that require a high level of core stability and require the central nervous system to send messages to the working muscle when muscles have been exhausted through cardiovascular exercise.

estimation of maximal oxygen uptake for men and women aged 20-69

HR	10	11	12	13	14	15	16	17	18	19	20
					Mins to walk a mile						
					men (20-29)						
120	65.0	61.7	58.4	55.2	51.9	48.6	45.4	42.1	38.9	35.6	32.3
130	63.4	60.1	56.9	53.6	50.3	47.1	43.8	40.6	37.3	34.0	30.8
140	61.8	58.6	55.3	52.0	48.8	45.5	42.2	39.0	35.7	32.5	29.2
150	60.3	57.0	53.7	50.5	47.2	43.9	40.7	37.4	34.2	30.9	27.6
160	58.7	55.4	52.2	48.9	45.6	42.4	39.1	35.9	32.6	29.3	26.1
170	57.1	53.9	50.6	57.3	44.1	40.8	37.6	34.3	31.0	27.8	24.5
180	55.6	52.3	49.0	45.8	42.5	39.3	36.0	32.7	29.5	26.2	22.9
190	54.0	50.7	47.5	44.2	41.0	37.7	34.4	31.2	27.9	24.6	21.4
200	52.4	49.2	45.9	42.7	39.4	36.1	32.9	29.6	26.3	23.1	19.8
					women (20-29)						
120	62.1	58.9	55.6	52.3	49.1	45.8	42.5	39.3	36.0	32.7	29.5
130	60.6	57.3	54.0	50.8	47.5	44.2	41.0	37.7	34.4	31.2	27.9
140	59.0	55.7	52.5	49.2	45.9	42.7	39.4	36.1	32.9	29.6	26.3
150	57.4	54.2	50.9	47.6	44.4	41.1	37.8	34.6	31.3	28.0	24.8
160	55.9	52.6	49.3	46.7	42.8	39.5	36.3	33.0	29.7	26.5	23.2
170	54.3	51.0	47.8	44.5	41.2	38.0	34.7	31.4	28.2	24.9	21.6
180	52.7	49.5	46.2	42.9	39.7	36.4	33.1	29.9	26.6	23.3	20.1
190	51.2	47.9	44.6	41.4	38.1	34.8	31.6	28.3	25.0	21.8	18.5
200	49.6	46.3	43.1	39.8	36.5	33.3	30.0	26.7	23.5	20.2	16.9
					men (30-39)						
120	61.1	57.8	54.6	51.3	48.0	44.8	41.5	38.2	35.0	31.7	28.4
130	59.5	56.3	53.0	49.7	46.5	43.2	39.9	36.7	33.4	20.1	26.9
140	58.0	54.7	51.4	48.2	44.9	41.6	38.4	35.1	31.8	28.6	25.3
150	56.4	53.1	49.9	46.6	43.3	40.1	36.8	33.5	30.0	27.0	23.8
160	54.8	51.6	48.3	45.0	41.8	38.5	35.2	32.0	28.7	25.5	22.2
170	53.3	50.0	46.7	43.5	40.2	36.9	33.7	30.4	27.1	23.9	20.6
180	51.7	48.4	45.2	41.9	38.6	35.4	32.1	28.8	25.6	22.3	19.1
190	50.1	46.9	43.6	40.3	37.1	33.8	30.5	27.3	24.0	20.8	17.5
					women (30-39)						
120	58.2	55.0	51.7	48.4	45.2	41.9	38.7	35.4	32.1	28.9	25.6
130	56.7	53.4	50.1	46.9	43.6	40.4	37.1	33.8	30.6	27.3	24.0
140	55.1	51.8	48.6	45.3	42.1	38.8	35.5	32.3	29.0	24.7	22.5
150	53.5	50.3	47.0	43.8	40.5	37.2	34.0	30.7	27.4	24.2	20.9
160	52.0	48.7	45.4	42.2	38.9	35.7	32.4	29.1	25.9	22.6	19.3
170	50.4	47.1	43.9	40.6	37.4	34.1	30.8	27.6	24.3	21.0	17.8
180	48.8	45.6	42.3	39.1	35.8	32.5	29.3	26.0	22.7	19.5	16.2
190	47.3	44.0	40.8	37.5	34.2	31.0	27.7	24.4	21.2	17.9	14.6

Table adapted from Howley and Franks (1997)

continues over page

estimation of maximal oxygen uptake for men and women aged 20-60 cont.

	Mins to walk a mile										
HR	**10**	**11**	**12**	**13**	**14**	**15**	**16**	**17**	**18**	**19**	**20**
					men (40-49)						
120	57.2	54.0	50.7	47.4	44.2	40.9	37.6	34.4	31.1	27.8	24.6
130	55.7	52.4	49.1	45.9	42.6	39.3	36.1	32.8	29.5	26.3	23.0
140	54.1	50.8	47.6	44.3	41.0	37.8	34.5	31.2	28.0	24.7	21.4
150	52.5	49.3	46.0	42.7	39.5	36.2	32.9	29.7	26.4	23.1	19.9
160	51.0	47.7	44.4	41.2	37.9	34.6	31.4	28.1	24.8	21.6	18.3
170	49.4	46.1	42.9	39.6	36.3	33.1	29.8	26.5	23.3	20.0	16.7
180	47.8	44.6	41.3	38.0	34.8	31.5	28.2	25.0	21.7	18.4	15.2
					women (40-49)						
120	54.4	51.1	47.8	44.6	41.3	38.0	34.8	31.5	28.2	25.0	21.7
130	52.8	49.5	46.3	43.0	39.7	36.5	33.2	29.9	26.7	23.4	20.1
140	51.2	48.0	46.3	43.0	39.7	36.5	33.2	29.9	26.7	23.4	20.1
150	49.7	46.4	43.1	39.9	36.6	33.3	30.1	26.8	23.5	20.3	17.0
160	48.1	44.8	41.6	38.3	35.0	31.8	28.5	25.2	22.0	18.7	15.5
170	46.5	43.3	40.0	36.7	33.5	30.2	26.9	23.7	20.4	17.2	13.9
					men (50-59)						
120	53.3	50.0	46.8	43.5	40.3	37.0	33.7	30.5	27.2	23.9	20.7
130	51.7	48.5	45.2	42.0	38.7	35.4	32.2	28.9	25.6	22.4	19.1
140	50.2	46.9	43.7	40.4	37.1	33.9	30.6	27.3	24.1	20.8	17.5
150	48.6	45.4	42.1	38.8	35.6	32.3	29.0	25.8	22.5	19.2	16.0
160	47.1	43.8	40.5	37.3	34.0	30.7	27.5	24.2	20.9	17.7	14.4
170	45.4	42.2	29.0	35.7	32.4	29.2	25.9	22.6	19.4	16.1	12.8
					women (50-59)						
120	50.5	47.2	43.9	40.7	37.4	34.1	30.9	27.6	24.3	21.1	17.8
130	48.9	45.6	42.4	39.1	35.8	32.6	29.3	26.0	22.8	19.5	16.2
140	47.3	44.1	40.8	37.5	34.3	31.0	27.7	24.5	21.2	17.9	4.7
150	45.8	42.5	9.2	36.0	32.7	29.4	26.2	2.9	19.6	16.4	13.1
160	44.2	40.9	37.7	34.4	31.1	27.9	24.6	21.3	18.1	14.8	11.5
170	42.6	39.4	36.1	32.8	29.6	26.3	23.0	19.8	16.5	13.2	10.0
					men (60-69)						
120	49.4	46.2	42.9	39.6	36.4	33.1	29.8	26.6	23.3	20.0	16.8
130	47.9	44.6	41.3	38.1	34.8	31.5	28.3	25.0	21.7	18.5	15.2
140	46.3	43.0	39.8	36.5	33.2	30.0	26.7	23.4	20.2	16.9	13.6
150	44.7	41.5	38.2	34.9	31.7	28.4	25.1	21.9	18.6	15.3	12.1
160	43.2	39.9	36.6	33.4	30.1	26.8	23.6	20.3	17.0	13.8	10.5
					women (60-69)						
120	46.6	43.3	40.0	36.8	33.5	30.2	27.0	23.7	20.5	17.2	13.9
130	45.0	41.7	38.5	35.2	31.9	28.7	25.4	22.2	18.9	15.6	12.4
140	43.4	40.2	36.9	33.6	30.4	27.1	23.8	20.6	17.3	14.1	10.8
150	41.9	38.6	35.3	32.1	28.8	25.5	22.3	19.0	15.8	12.5	9.2
160	40.3	37.0	33.8	30.5	27.2	24,0	20.7	17.5	14.2	10.9	7.7

the jog or run test

There are two main running tests that can be employed to assess your cardiovascular capacity. These are the 1.5 mile (2.4km) run and the 12-minute run. Both of these tests were designed for use on a running track. You can get a rough approximation if you run on different terrain or on a treadmill instead.

For the 1.5 mile run test you must run the 1.5 miles as quickly as you can and must record the total time taken to complete the distance. Compare your score with the table below, according to your age and sex.

For the 12-minute run, you must run or jog as far as you can in 12 minutes. Once again, compare your score to the table below, according to your age and sex, to compare your stamina against the average.

For both tests ensure that:

1 You have used the ACSM Risk Stratification Table (see page 26) to ensure that you are fit.
2 You have completed an initial conditioning phase as set out by the ACSM.
3 You have completed a thorough warm up prior to the test.
4 You are thoroughly hydrated.

estimation of maximal oxygen uptake for men and women aged 20-69

age	**units of stamina**		**1.5-mile run (mins)**		**12-minute run (miles)**		
	female	male	female	male	female	male	
15-30	> 40	> 45	< 12	< 10	> 1.5	> 1.7	**good**
35-50	> 35	> 40	< 13:30	< 11:30	> 1.4	> 1.5	
55-70	> 30	> 35	< 6	< 14	> 1.2	> 1.3	
15-30	35	40	13:30	11:50	1.4	1.5	**adequate for most activities**
35-50	30	35	15	13	1.3	1.4	
55-70	25	30	17:30	15:30	1.1	1.3	
15-30	30	35	15	13	1.3	1.4	**borderline**
35-50	25	30	16:30	14:30	1.2	1.3	
55-70	20	25	19	17	1.0	1.2	
15-30	> 25	> 30	> 17	> 15	< 1.2	< 1.3	**needs more work on aerobic fitness**
35-50	> 20	> 25	> 18:30	> 16:30	< 1.1	< 1.2	
55-70	> 15	> 20	> 21	> 19	< 0.9	< 1.1	

chapter 4

developing a cardiovascular training session

- warm up
- endurance phase
- cool down

mobilization and stretches

- common areas of muscular dysfunction
- mid-upper back self-assessment
- mid-upper back mobilization
- calf stretch
- standing thigh stretch
- quad and hip flexor stretch
- forward bow
- bent leg hamstring stretch
- hip flexor and oblique stretch
- lower-back stretch
- glute stretch
- forward floor lean
- TFL stretch
- gluteus medius stretch
- pec minor stretch

postural exercises

- inverted breathing pattern test
- mckenzie press
- alternate superman
- full superman
- prone cobra
- four-point prone exercise
- pelvic rock

warm up

A cardiovascular training session can be broken down into three main components: the warm up, the endurance phase, and the cool down. You should warm up and cool down before and after any physical activity from gardening to sailing, running to mountaineering.

The purpose of the warm up is to prepare you psychologically and physiologically for more vigorous exercise. The transition from resting to moderate to vigorous exercise should be gradual. This allows your blood pressure and heart rate to rise in a controlled manner.

The warm up also means that both your postural muscles and the muscles responsible for gross movement become accustomed to what is to follow. This promotes joint flexibility and overall range of motion, and may prevent injury. The warm up should be composed of stretches for those major muscle groups that will be used in the exercises and a light aerobic mobilization warm up.

Stretching should target the main muscles you will use in your session. For example, a runner should stretch the hamstrings, calves, glutes, and thigh muscles, while a canoeist should focus on the upper body, targeting the obliques, back, chest, and shoulders.

The light aerobic warm up should last 5–10 minutes and should prepare the body for the endurance phase of the session. Consider the principle of specificity when you are warming up. It makes very little sense warming up on the bike if the main part of your endurance session is running! Note that in all of your exercises, you should inhale just before, and exhale just as you execute each stage.

below > **Adapt your warm up routine to the type of exercise you are about to set out on. Running requires a thorough warming up of the leg muscles.**

endurance phase

If you are doing cardiovascular training for general health and fitness the ACSM recommends 20 to 60 minutes of continuous or interval aerobic exercise. If you are involved in more athletic training, you may need to exercise for longer. If you are a complete beginner, you may start with whatever period of training you can comfortably manage. Select your endurance phase exercises from those on pages 82–127.

right > **A combination of jogging and walking is a good way of alternating your endurance exercise as a beginner trainer. It allows you to adapt the exercise according to your fitness level.**

pointers for endurance training

- Listen to your body. If you are in pain or distress, wind down the training to a level that feels comfortable.
- Build up gradually. Improvement will rapidly become evident, motivating you to the next level of endurance.
- Never compare. Don't try to match what other people are achieving. Only you know what feels right for you.
- Try to maintain a level of exercise that exerts you, without over-exerting yourself. Check your pulse frequently to make sure that your heart rate falls within your heart-rate training zone (see page 34) instead of below or above it.

cool down

The cool down is just as important as the warm up and endurance phases. Its purpose is to provide a safe, gradual decrease from the elevated intensity of exercise. There are many times in the gym when I have seen somebody slumped over the treadmill after completing an exhaustive run.

Given that during intense exercise the heart rate shoots up to nearly 200 bpm, the last thing you want to do is stay still while your heart attempts to pump blood around the body. If you do, you'll be a prime candidate for a heart attack.

You may cool down by gradually decreasing the intensity of your exercise. As a rule of thumb, after cardiovascular exercise you should wait until your heart rate is below 110 bpm. This will ensure that your blood pressure returns to near pre-exercise levels without any dangerous sudden fluctuations.

below > **A wind down does not mean slumping over the equipment as soon as you've finished your exercise! Attempt to cool down actively, not statically.**

mobilization and stretches

Having an adequate range of movement is key to participating in cardiovascular exercise. Without it, you will not perform any activity effectively and your progress may be limited. If you can develop an understanding of which of your muscles are long and weak or short and tight, you can develop an individual stretching routine that is appropriate to your needs.

If you find it difficult to stretch, it may be advisable to see a corrective exercise specialist. If you carry on regardless, you may find that your range of motion becomes even more limited and more often than not you'll suffer from pain. The following mobilization exercises and stretches are designed to work specific muscle groups that commonly cause trouble. They should form part of your warm up.

In general, stretches should:

- not be painful, though they may feel uncomfortable
- not cause shaking of the muscles
- target the muscles that are short and tight
- improve the range of motion at the specific joints used in the exercise
- be held for at least 20 to 30 seconds.

below > **An exercise specialist can help you understand the nuances of your body: any limitations, stiffness, or bad habits that need to be corrected.**

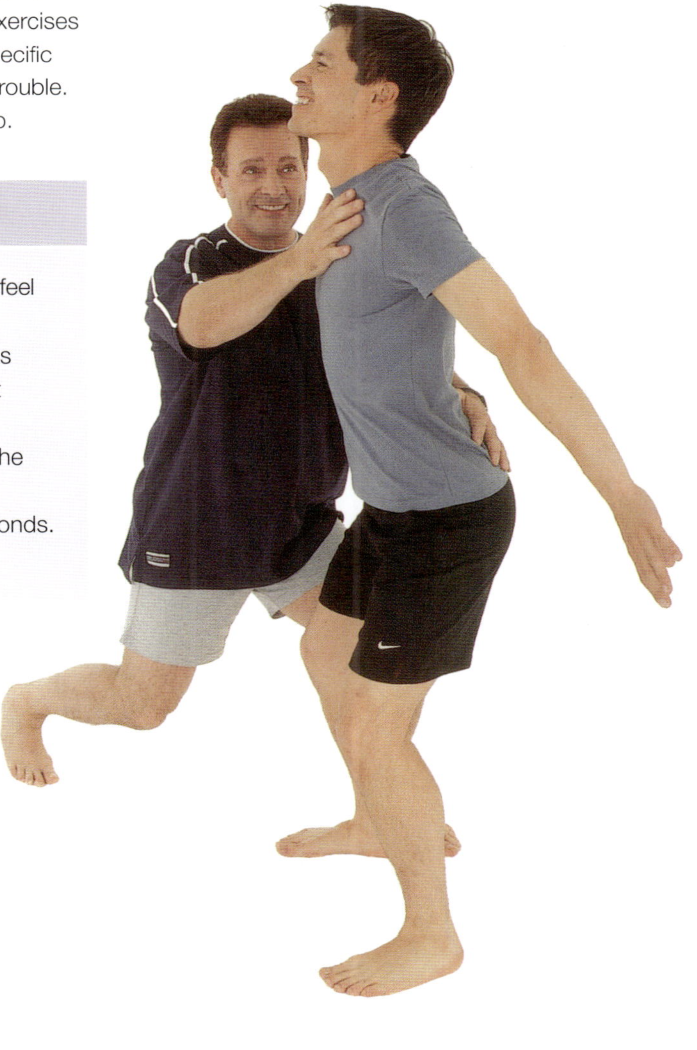

common areas of muscular dysfunction

These areas of the body are particularly susceptible to problems. You are most likely to feel pain, stiffness, or a lack of mobility in these muscles, so concentrate on them when doing the stretches and mobilization exercises that follow.

mid–upper back

The thoracic or midsection of the spine often becomes dysfunctional due to long periods of inactivity, such as sitting at a desk in front of a computer all day, or due to participation in inappropriate exercise, for example performing hundreds of sit-ups. Having a dysfunctional spine can affect the way we breathe and move, while having an optimal spine position is necessary for correct exercise.

lower back

The erector spinae muscles of the lower back are the muscles that are responsible for returning the back from a forward flexed position into an upright one. Depending on the position of the pelvis these muscles can become short and tight or long and weak. Some of the following exercises help to restore the lumbar or lower-back curve, which should ideally be between 30 and 35 degrees.

abdominal muscles

The lower abdominal muscles play a major role in stabilizing the lower limbs but they are often weak. This is because the hip flexors can take over their work, making the lower abdominal muscles short, which rotates the pelvis and may eventually cause back pain.

Many people suffer from a de-conditioning of the deep abdominal wall (transversus abdominus). If you are a woman who has been pregnant, this muscle will have stretched. If you are a couch potato, chances are it will have been a long time since you have used it at all! Fortunately, anyone can retrain their deep abdominal wall. We should be able to switch it on and off unconsciously when it is needed to help stabilize the spine, for example when picking a heavy object up off the floor. It is especially important for sports people who need this muscle to be strong to brace the spine during contact or when being tackled.

lower back muscles

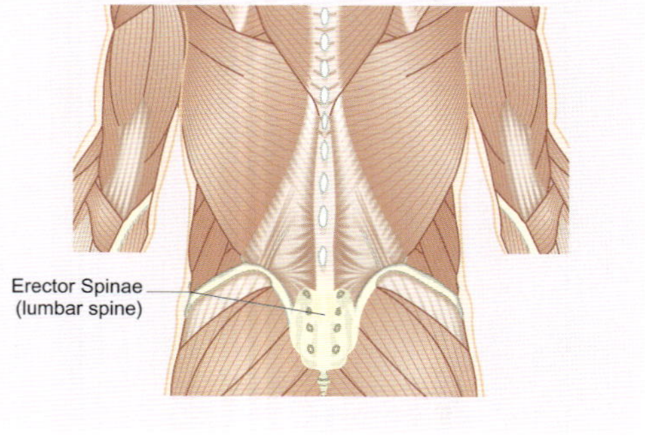

abdominal muscles

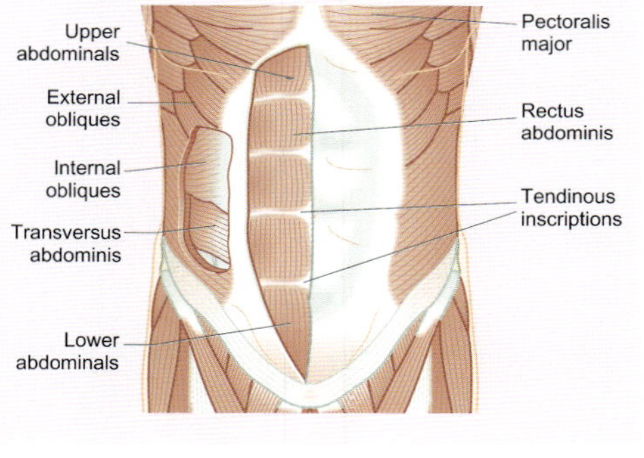

front of thigh

The quadriceps are the large muscles on the front of the thigh and, like the calf muscles, they are used whenever we walk, run, stand up, or sit down. The rectus femoris—a muscle of the quadriceps—together with the hip flexor muscle is prone to tightening and can cause a forward rotation of the pelvis which affects the mechanics of locomotion and may cause lower-back pain. Some of the following exercises stretch both of these muscles and are particularly effective in preventing this from happening.

inner thigh

The inner thighs or adductors are a series of muscles that run from above the knee all the way up toward the pelvis. They play a particularly important role in stabilizing the body during walking and running.

hamstrings

The hamstrings are the muscles at the back of the thighs. Tight hamstrings usually mean a flat lower back and if left unchecked, can cause a backward rotation of the pelvis and lower-back pain. This can often be seen in the sedentary office worker or in people who are repetitive single-mode exercisers, such as runners or cyclists. The hamstrings can be stretched in a variety of ways, but I prefer the forward bow (page 63) and the bent leg hamstring stretch (page 64).

calf muscles

The calf muscles are subjected to stress whenever we walk, run, stand up, or sit down. Ideally, these muscles should be stretched daily, especially in the case of women who wear high-heeled shoes, since these restrict normal movement of the calf muscles and tend to shorten and tighten them.

The calf muscle is made up of two large muscles. The larger, bulky part of the calf is called the gastrocnemius, or gastroc, and the longer, slender, lower part of the calf is called the soleus. It is important to stretch both of these muscles as part of a stretching routine in order to achieve an adequate range of motion at the ankle joint.

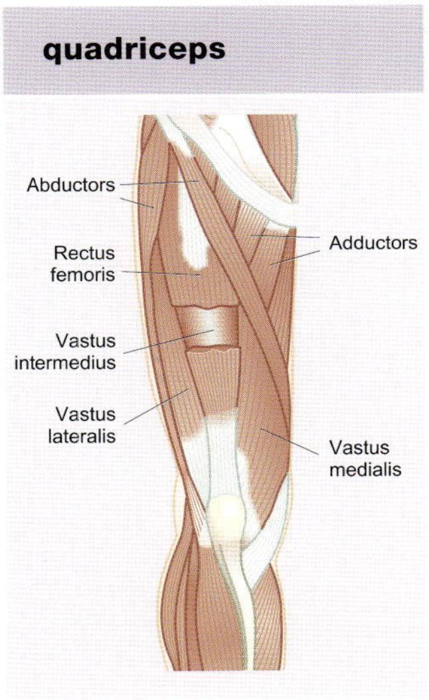

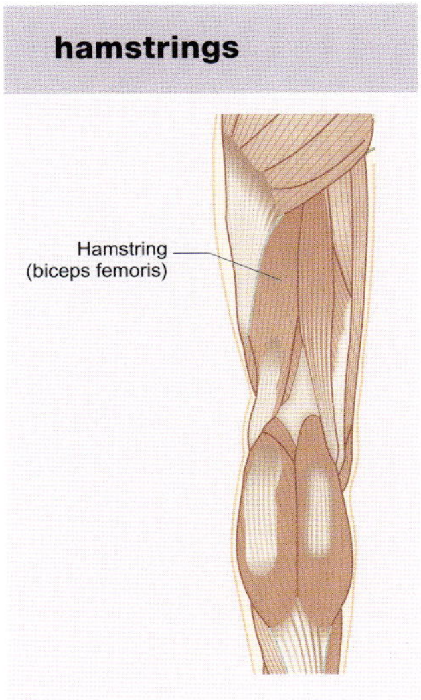

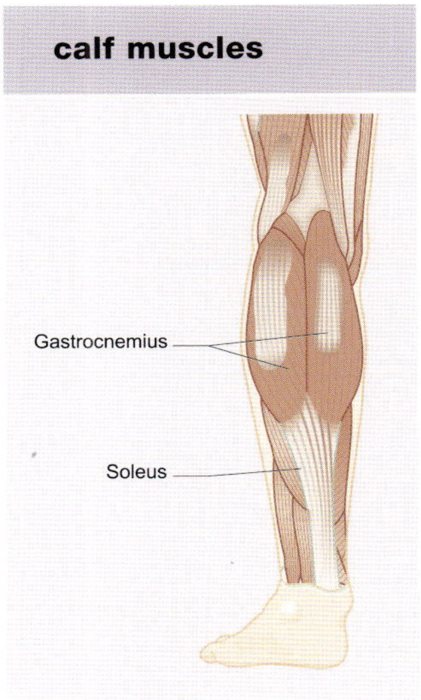

mid–upper back self-assessment

If you are unsure whether you have an adequate range of motion in your mid–upper back, try this simple thoracic spine flexibility test.

1 Stand with the back to a wall, heels at least 6 inches (15cm) away from the wall and the palms of the hands facing forward.

2 Raise the arms above the head. Feel or use a mirror to see whether your mid–upper back comes away from the wall. If there is a gap, this means that you lack sufficient mid-back flexibility. If the gap is significant (more than a couple of inches/centimeters), you may need to see a corrective exercise or back specialist prior to doing a mid–upper back mobilization.

mid–upper back mobilization

This exercise helps to restore correct spinal alignment along the length of the mid–upper back. Mobilization is particularly important in order to achieve an adequate range of motion during the stretching element of your warm up.

1 Lie on your back on the floor and place a foam roller or a rolled towel crosswise beneath your mid-back. Support the neck with your hands.

2 Gently roll your spine backward and the hips down so the roller moves up the back. Lie there for 3 to 6 seconds. Repeat 2 to 3 times to move the roller to different sections of the spine.

tips

- **Ensure you do not roll onto the neck.**
- **Always roll off the roller to the side before standing up, otherwise you will undo all your good work.**

calf stretch

The calf muscles are often tight and need stretching on a daily basis.

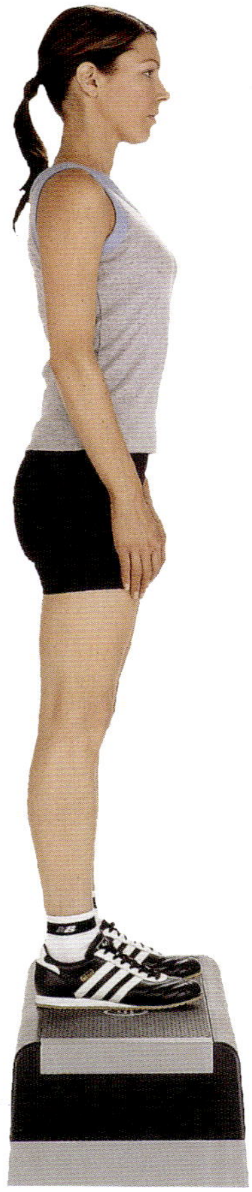

1 Stand on a low step with your arms hanging loosely by your sides.

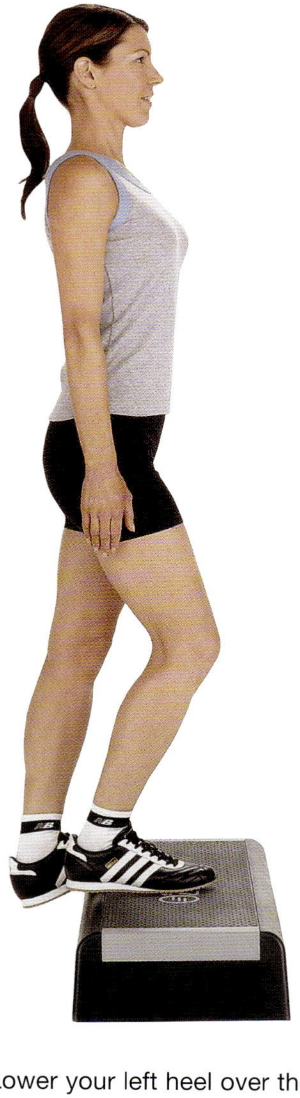

2 Lower your left heel over the edge of the step, bending the right knee slightly. Drop your body weight down onto the left calf muscle. Hold for a few seconds to feel the full magnitude of the stretch.

3 Add a little more body weight to increase the stretch. Return to the start position, then repeat with the other leg.

standing thigh stretch

The front of the thigh can be prone to shortening or lengthening. For short tight muscles, stretch, but for long weak muscles, it may not be necessary.

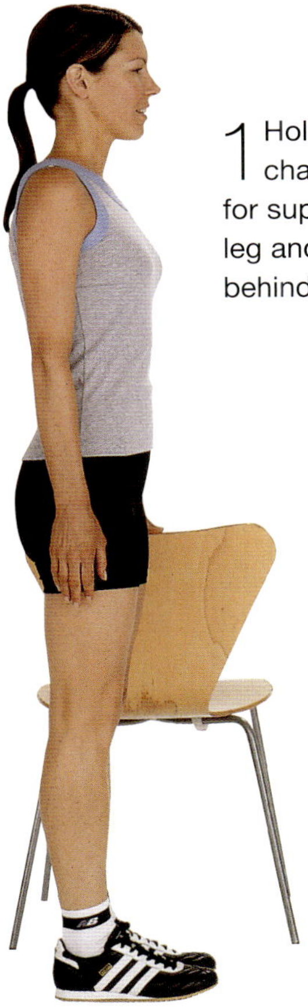

1 Holding the back of a chair or something similar for support, stand on the left leg and bring the right leg up behind you.

tip

- If you have really short, tight hip flexors you may need to work through a smaller range of motion initially. The heel should be able to touch the backside to indicate a adequate range of motion.

2 Grab the right ankle and slowly draw the right heel up toward the buttocks. Repeat on the other side.

quad and hip flexor stretch

As your range of motion develops, try using a Swiss ball to develop hip and thigh flexibility even more.

tip

- If you feel unstable, stand near a wall and use it to help you balance.

1 Kneel in a split-leg position with a Swiss ball behind you. The left foot should be on the floor in front and the right knee resting on the floor behind you. Keeping the left leg bent, place the right foot on the ball.

variation

- You can move the front leg backward or forward to increase or decrease the amount of stretch.

2 Slowly bend the left leg further forward over the foot until you can feel the stretch in the quads of the right leg. Hold for 30–60 seconds, then repeat with the left leg resting on the ball.

forward bow

This exercise is particularly effective for stretching the hamstrings at the back of the thigh, and is also beneficial for the lower back muscles.

1 Stand with legs straight, feet together, and arms crossed over the chest.

tip

- Do not allow the back to flatten out by bending too far forward.

2 Slowly bend forward from the hips until you feel a stretch in the back of the thighs. Hold for 30–60 seconds.

bent leg hamstring stretch

This exercise gives a stretch higher up the back of the thigh.

1 Kneel on a mat on the floor in a split-leg position, with the right knee in front and the left knee resting on the floor behind you.

2 Attempt to straighten the right leg until you feel the stretch in the hamstrings. Hold for 30–60 seconds then repeat on the other side.

tip

- Keep the hands on the thighs for balance.

hip flexor and oblique stretch

The obliques are responsible for twisting and flexing the trunk but they also work to decelerate the pelvis during running and sprinting activities. They sometimes become short and tight. This is a multi-muscle stretch that helps the flexibility of the pelvis and the trunk.

1 Kneel on a mat on the floor in a split-leg position, with the right foot on the floor and the left knee resting on the floor behind you. Raise the arms over the head and use the left hand to hold the right arm at the elbow, as in the picture.

2 Take your body weight toward the right knee while pressing the left knee into the mat and lifting the upper trunk away from the left hip.

3 Hold for 30–60 seconds, then repeat on the other side.

lower-back stretch

The back muscles are particularly prone to dysfunction. If they are short and tight, they will restrict your movement and if they are weak, they may allow excessive movement. Either way, you are sure to suffer some back pain. If your lower back muscles, or erector spinae, are long and weak there is little point in trying to stretch them further. If however, they are short and tight, you should stretch them prior to exercise.

1 Lie face up on a mat on the floor. Breathe in and, as you do so, grab both knees.

2 Breathe out, then pull your knees in toward your chest and hold for at least 30 seconds.

glute stretch

The glutes are the muscles of the buttocks and are essential for extending the hip joint. If they become tight, it can lead to a flat back. During repetitive cardiovascular exercise such as running and cycling, the glutes are needed for extending and straightening the hip joint. They may need stretching before and after each bout of exercise.

1 Lie face up on a mat on the floor. Rotate the right thigh to the right, then breathe in as you place the right ankle on the left leg above the left knee.

2 Breathe out and, as you do so, draw the left leg in toward your chest until you feel a stretch in the buttocks. Hold for at least 30 seconds. Repeat using the other leg.

forward floor lean

This is particularly effective for stretching the inner thighs and glutes.

1 Kneel on all fours on a mat, resting on the forearms.

2 Breathe in and as you breathe out drop further forward onto the forearms while pushing back into the thighs.

tip

- Attempt this stretch gradually as it has a habit of kicking in after 5 to 10 seconds. If you do not feel enough stretch, take the legs slightly farther apart and gradually push back into the thighs again.

variation

- Once your legs are apart and you have got used to the stretch, try moving your body backward, to increase the stretch.

TFL stretch

The outer thigh muscles, or abductors, help to move the leg away from the midline of the body during the swing in the recovery phase when walking and running. The following stretch works one of the specific muscles of this group—the tensor fascia latae (TFL).

1 Standing with the right side of the body parallel to a wall, bend the left knee over the right leg and rest the right forearm or elbow on the wall.

2 Keeping the right leg straight, breathe in and, as you exhale, lean forward from the hips until you feel a stretch running down the outside of the left thigh. Hold for 30–60 seconds. Repeat on the other side.

gluteus medius stretch

The gluteus medius muscles in the buttocks are, along with the tensor fascia latae (TFL) muscle, responsible for taking the thighs away from the body when walking and running.

1 Lying flat on your back on a mat on the floor, keep the left leg straight as you take the right leg over the left and rest the heel of the right foot on the floor. Use the left hand to grab the right leg just above the knee.

tip

- The stretch should feel as though it is coming from the outer, more lateral part of the backside.

2 Breathe in and as you breathe out, pull the right thigh across the body. You should feel the stretch in the outer left thigh. Hold for at least 30 seconds. Repeat on the other side.

pec minor stretch

The pectoralis minor is a muscle of the chest that assists the diaphragm when we breathe in by drawing the ribs upward and elevating the rib cage. Given that successful cardiovascular exercise is dependent on the rate of breathing, it is particularly important that the muscles involved in breathing should not be short and tight.

1 Kneel on a mat on all fours with a Swiss ball next to you on the right.

2 Take the right arm out 90 degrees and bend the right elbow to a 90-degree angle, resting it on the ball.

3 Breathe in and as you breathe out apply your body weight to the elbow gradually so that the shoulder joint is pushed simultaneously backward and upward. Hold for 30 seconds, then repeat on the other side.

postural exercises

"Posture is the beginning and ending point of all movement. If you begin in the wrong place, you'll most likely end in the wrong place!" These are the words of Paul Chek of the C.H.E.K. Institute in California and you should bear them in mind as your mantra.

The postural muscles (see page 17) are those that maintain the position of the musculo-skeletal system for long periods of time. Postural muscles have a predominance of type 1 fibers that are either aerobic or cardiovascular. They have endurance-type qualities and respond well to specific exercises. Exercising for long periods of time in a sport such as long distance running can increase the likelihood of muscle dysfunction. In other words, certain muscles become short and strong while their antagonists become long and weak. Runners, in particular, often suffer from excessive rounding of the upper back muscles. This increases hamstring tension and rotates the pelvis, restricting the individual to less than optimal performance and creating the possibility of injury.

Sedentary workers can develop muscular dysfunction as well as regular exercisers. Many have a flat back—the lower back muscles are over-long and weak. This is known as lumbar flexion syndrome (a and b).

The commonly named "sway back" is correctly called kyphosis lordosis. Short, tight muscles in the thigh, hip, and lower back cause forward rotation of the pelvis (lordosis), while short, tight abdominal muscles round the upper back and shoulders (kyphosis). You can often also see the head carried too far forward (c).

Such postural problems lead to pain, expend more of the body's energy, and cause injury. In the case of exercisers, poor posture prevents them from completing good quality exercise. So what is good posture?

When someone is standing correctly, it should be possible to run an imaginary plumb line running between the ankle, knee, hip,

a

shoulder, and ear. This is known as neutral spine and is the point at which all the muscles that support, stabilize, and contribute to movement are at their optimal length (d).

A neutral spine should be the primary objective for all who exercise as it will ensure they remain free from injury and back pain.

If you are a regular exerciser it is important that you exercise with good posture in order to stay injury-free. Aerobically training the postural muscles will help you achieve that. If you are doing any of the programs in chapter 6, it is best to perform the following postural exercises at the end or you will be too tired to get through the program.

The exercises recommended here should not be done if you suffer from any back pain. If your are in any doubt what shape your spine is in, seek the advice of a corrective exercise specialist, osteopath, or chiropractor.

b c d

inverted breathing pattern test

Correct breathing is essential to help prevent muscular dysfunction in the respiratory muscles, and so prevent pain in the neck and lower back which may prevent you from exercising over extended periods of time. Incorrect breathing is known as "inverted breathing." This exercise checks for and helps correct inverted breathing.

1 Stand as normal. Place one hand on your chest and the other on the navel. Take a breath in through your nose and observe the movement that occurs at the chest and the navel. You should feel the first two-thirds of the movement in the area of the navel and the last third in the chest. If this doesn't occur, repeat the breath in repetitions of ten, concentrating on achieving the correct breathing pattern.

tip

- Remember that an incorrect, or inverted, breathing pattern will have developed over thousands of hours of repetition, so you won't be able to correct it immediately.

mckenzie press

This mobilization exercise should be done as part of the warm up or mobilization part of your session—it will mobilize the lower back. You can also do it as part of your cool down.

1 Lie face down on a mat with your hands beneath your shoulders, then breathe in.

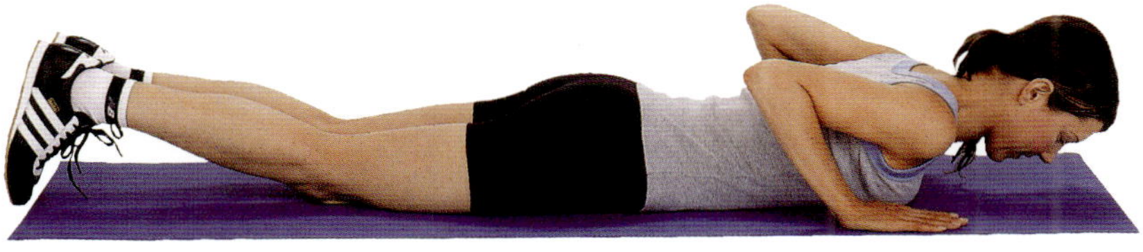

2 Breathe out as you push upward, ensuring that the bony part of the pelvis stays in contact with the floor. Hold for a second then lower. Repeat 10 times.

tip

- The tempo for the exercise should be: one second up, one second hold, and one second to lower.

alternate superman

This is particularly effective for helping to strengthen the muscles of the lumbar and thoracic back.

1 Lie face down on a mat with the arms stretched over the head a little more than hip-width apart and the thumbs pointing upward.

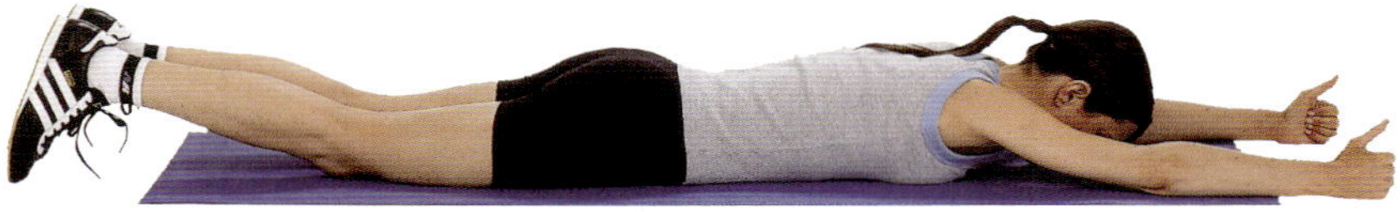

2 Raise the right arm and the left leg off the floor to approximately the same height. Hold for 5 to 10 seconds, breathing out as you do so.

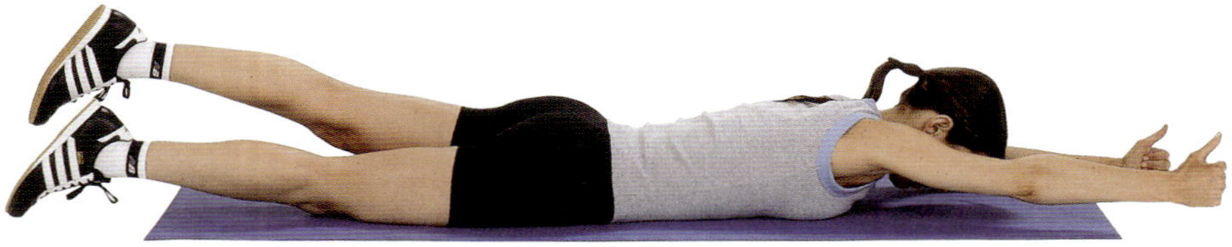

3 Repeat using the other arm and leg, then rest for 10 seconds. Repeat 5 to 10 times.

full superman

This helps to restore lumbar curvature and the mid-back extensors at the same time. Consider this exercise a progression from the alternate superman.

1 Lie face down on a mat with your arms stretched over your head and the thumbs pointing upward.

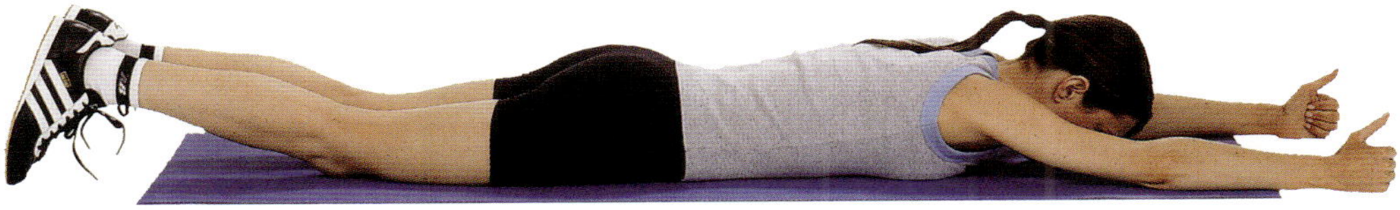

2 Ensuring that your thumbs point upward, raise the arms and legs simultaneously approximately 45 degrees off the floor. Hold for 10 seconds, breathing out as you do so. Rest for 10 seconds.

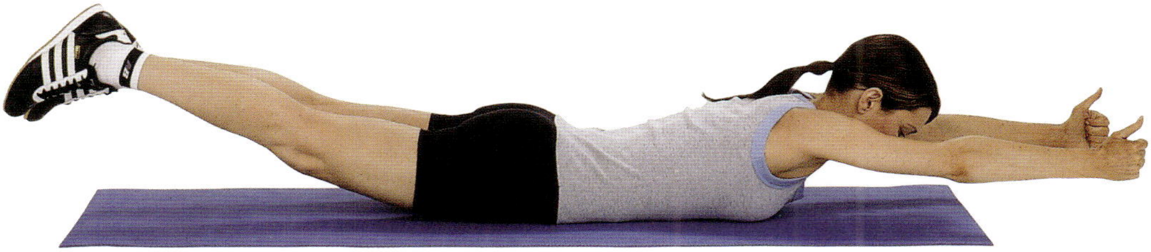

tip

- **Ask a "spotter" or helper to check that you are symmetrical.**

3 Repeat 2 to 3 times. Try working up to 10 repetitions of 2 to 3 sets.

prone cobra

This exercise works the thoracic erectors and is the most effective exercise for restoring the correct curve to the back. It should be considered an integral part of any conditioning program for people with lumbar flexion syndrome (see page 72). It should always come at the end of the program as it places a great demand on the muscles of the mid and lower back if the glutes are involved.

1 Lie face down on a mat with your arms down by your sides alongside the body, palms facing the ceiling.

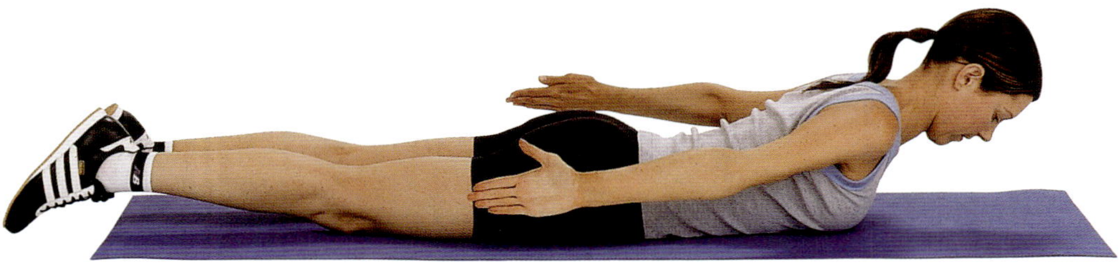

2 Using the back muscles, raise your chest off the floor, simultaneously rotating the arms so the palms face outwards. Keep the chin tucked in. Hold for 10 seconds.

3 Rest for 10 seconds then repeat. Try working up to 10 repetitions, then progress to a 1, 2, and finally a 3-minute hold.

tip

- **If you have excessive curvature in the lower back, contract your glutes before you lift your chest.**

four-point prone exercise

This exercise helps to target the Transversus Abdominis muscle, which plays a significant role in stabailizing the spine under load. Lower back pain can be lessened when this muscle is conditioned appropriately in conjunction with a stretching and strengthening program.

1 Kneel on hands and knees on a mat on the floor. Ensure that the knees are directly below the hips and that the hands are directly below the shoulders.

2 Keep the chin tucked in and face the floor, then bend the elbows slightly and have a "spotter" or helper place a pole along the length of the spine. The spotter should check that the pole makes contact with your spine in three places—at the hip, mid-back and head.

3 On an exhalation, draw the navel in toward the spine. Hold for 10 seconds.

4 Relax for 10 seconds then repeat. Complete 10 repetitions and 3 sets.

tip

• There should be no movement in the back. All the work should come from the abdomen. If you find it hard to hold for 10 seconds, try for 5 then work up.

variation

• Progress the exercise by attempting it in a bent-over position.

pelvic rock

This helps to work the lower abdominal muscles without using the hip flexors.

1 Lie on the floor on your back with legs bent and feet flat on the floor. Place one hand, palm face up, under the lower back, roughly beneath the navel.

2 Rotate the pelvis backward until you can feel pressure on your fingers. Hold for 10 seconds, then relax for 10 seconds.

3 Work toward holding the contraction for 2 minutes.

tip

• If you are not sure which muscles should be working, place the other hand on top of your body, just below the navel. You can then feel if the lower abdominal muscles contract when you rotate the pelvis.

variation

- Leaving one foot on the floor, raise the other as you perform the pelvic rock. Repeat on the other side.

- Take both legs off the floor as you perform the pelvic rock.

chapter 5

endurance phase exercise

cardiovascular exercise

- walking
- running and jogging
- cycling
- water-based cardiovascular exercise
- aerobics classes

cardiovascular training in the gym

- the cycle
- the treadmill
- the elliptical cross trainer
- the rowing machine

general body conditioning

- the lunge
- multi-point lunge
- twisties
- hamstring kicks
- wood chop with medicine ball
- reverse chop
- dead lift
- lateral jumps
- step-ups
- step-overs
- ball balances
- hip extensions
- half push-ups
- upright row
- bent-over row
- squat and press
- tricep dips
- back extensions with ball

cardiovascular exercise

Cardiovascular exercise is any physical activity that increases the heart rate, increases the rate of respiration, increases body temperature, and increases the amount of fats and carbohydrates used for energy synthesis.

It involves movements that use the large muscles in the body that depend on oxygen to function for extended periods of time. As a corrective and holistic exercise coach, I recommend using gyms and fitness centers for establishing correct movement patterns and for training development. However, for cardiovascular exercise I thoroughly recommend exercising outdoors, particularly in the countryside, where the air is relatively clean compared to polluted city roads. Exercising in areas of natural beauty also helps to reduce general stress levels, even if you are just taking a brisk walk. If you train outdoors in a busy city environment, try to follow these guidelines if possible:

- Avoid running/cycling along any roads where pollution levels are high.

- Try to train along river or canal tracks, or in city parks.

- For night-time exercise, always run in areas that are well lit and frequented by other exercisers.

walking

Walking, running, and jogging all use the muscles responsible for locomotion or movement. This repetitive movement requires the use of the oxidative system (see pages 14–17) in order to be maintained over longer periods of time. Brisk walking allows the use of fat as the main source of energy and produces a high level of calorific expenditure.

When you are new to exercise, try walking on flattish terrain to begin with. You will find that walking for as little as 20 minutes can bring significant health benefits. As you develop cardiovascular fitness and muscular strength, try walking off-road in the country where the terrain will be less even. This will help load the stabilizing muscles of the legs and trunk and can provide a refreshing change from treadmill training in a sweaty gym. Walking uphill creates a greater workload on the glutes or muscles of the buttocks. Walking downhill places greater emphasis on the quads or front of the thighs. Because it involves a lengthening rather than a shortening of the working muscles, you may experience considerable soreness after a lot of downhill walking.

Power walking is a variation of walking in which you use larger rhythmical movements of the shoulder, hip, and knee joints to increase your speed.

You often see people using hand and ankle weights when walking in the gym, but although the added weight increases the amount of calories used in a session, it should be avoided. The demand placed on the knee, hip, and shoulder joints can cause severe injuries to the joint and its surrounding ligaments and tendons.

The actions of walking, jogging, and running are very similar. For each movement there are three phases: push off, recovery, and landing. As a rule, at the landing phase, the heel should strike the ground first. If you increase the pace to running, the ball of the foot comes into contact with the ground first.

running and jogging

Running is a very effective way of developing cardiovascular fitness, but people often go straight into it without following a light walking program as part of their pre-running training. Depending on the surface that you train on, running can be particularly stressful on the knee joints and can cause injury if you are not careful.

As you develop cardiovascular fitness and start to train at intensities above 80 percent of your stamina, there is an increased incidence of injury to the bones and connective tissues as well. Treadmill running can be an appropriate place to start running as the loads on the joints are less, although some people find the experience of treadmill work slightly disorientating. Running outside, particularly on concrete, should only be attempted after appropriate conditioning. Some find running on grass slightly less stressful than road running. The less stable the surface under your feet, for example when running on sand or mud, the greater the load on the postural muscles. If the surface is very unstable, you can strain your back. People who already have back problems should try to avoid running on an unstable surface.

right > **When jogging always ensure you wear bright, ideally reflective, gear. This will alert other road users to your presence and increase your safety.**

far right > **When cycling, whether in a city or in the countryside, always wear a proper cycling helmet. They are essential for safety and could save your life.**

cycling

This is a great way to train the cardiovascular system and clock up relatively large distances. Because it is a non-impact exercise, it is effective and safe for people with problems in the leg joints and back. Cycling outdoors poses significant problems in areas of high traffic.

Firstly, there is the threat of injury through accident. Secondly, dense traffic means high levels of carbon monoxide, which limits cardiovascular capacity by binding to blood cells and restricting the amount of oxygen that can be delivered to the working tissues. If you have to cycle in heavy traffic, you should wear a suitable mask.

Mountain or cross-country biking is a great way of cycling in spectacular surroundings. The terrain will offer varying levels of exercise intensity and this exercise beats cycling on a stationary cycle in the gym any day. Cycling in difficult terrain poses obvious problems so ensure that you have the right safety equipment and most importantly, start off at the right level. Don't try cycling up Ben Nevis at your first attempt and always let someone know where you are cycling, especially if you are on your own and attempting a stretch of terrain that you have never cycled before. If you wear your heart-rate monitor as you cycle, you will be able to assess the level of difficulty of your uphill work.

water-based cardiovascular exercise

Water-based exercise offers safe and effective training for anyone with joint problems as the water takes a significant load away from the supporting joints. It can be a particularly good choice for people who are undertaking a course of rehabilitation.

Walking or running across the pool or in the ocean requires a higher calorific expenditure than walking or running on dry land. It also provides a way of training without the usual risk of injuries that can be caused by these types of impact exercise.

Swimming is another great way of training the cardiovascular system without the bumps and stress of impact exercise. Like many other forms of exercise, it uses a variety of joints but you can change your swimming style to involve slightly different muscle groups. The overall training effect will be dictated by the amount of time you spend swimming, so if you practice sprint swimming, such as 100 meters, you will develop your short-term energy system. To train the cardiovascular system, you should start by attempting to swim for longer than 3 minutes. If you are not comfortable with your swimming technique, try using floats to get started, or take some lessons to increase your confidence.

- **Front crawl:** Here the shoulders and larger back muscles are used along with the kicking action of the legs to create forward motion.

- **Breaststroke:** This requires the use of the back and chest muscles with a lot of the leg work coming from the inner and outer thighs.

aerobics classes

The huge increase in the number of health clubs has seen a rise in the variety of aerobics classes on offer. There is something to suit every different fitness level, age, and ability.

- **General:** these classes are designed to elevate the heart rate by involving most of the major muscles. Classes vary in level from beginner to advanced and usually the rate of progression is dictated by the complexity of choreographed moves and routines.

- **Step:** This was one of the most popular classes to come into the aerobic studio in the last decade. A step, set at various heights depending on your fitness levels, is used in combination with choreographed moves. This results in a greater level of energy expenditure due to the increased load placed on the thighs and muscles of the buttocks. Step classes can be quite demanding for the unconditioned person so try a general aerobics class first.

- **Body pump:** This has become very popular in the last few years and is based around conditioning using weights. The conditioning effect can be cardiovascular or strength-based depending on the intensity, the time that the muscles are under contraction (see page 17), and the rest period.

- **Aqua:** Water aerobics is particularly effective for those new to exercise or those who have some experience but are returning to exercise after an injury. The larger muscles are worked through the resistance of the water. The impact of normal standing activities is also lessened in the water and the muscles are not subject to as much stress as they would be on dry land.

cardiovascular training in the gym

These days it seems that you can't turn a corner without seeing a newly opened gym. Thankfully gym equipment is fairly generic and although there are a variety of brand names, the functions and programs tend to remain the same.

Most gym equipment, apart from machines like the rowing machine, have pre-designed programs that allow you to input individual variables such as:

- your weight, in order to assess calorific expenditure per minute or per hour
- the selected workload as an expression of speed in mph or kph
- proposed length of time for exercise
- your chosen heart-rate training zone.

Most machines also have a number of modes to provide variety and maintain motivation.

- **Fat Burn:** This mode offers low to moderate intensity exercise that uses fat as a fuel at a higher rate than carbohydrates.
- **Cardio Zone:** This mode is primarily concerned with the development of the cardiovascular system.

climate and exercise

Most gyms generally operate at 65–70°F (18–21°C). Temperatures above 77° F (25°C) can see dramatic changes in performance. If you have to exercise in the heat, consider the following points:

- attempt to let the body acclimatize to environmental temperature (up to 10 days)
- limit exercise to light sessions of 15 to 20 minutes initially
- increase intensity gradually
- increase fluid intake to cope with excessive amounts of sweat
- be aware of signs of dehydration
- if humidity is high, evaporation will be restricted and intensity should be reduced
- wear clothing that is light in color to reflect heat from sunlight
- continue to re-hydrate post-exercise
- water alone is not enough to replenish the essential minerals lost during exercise. Modern sports drinks often provide vitamins and minerals to assist with re-hydration.

Exercising in the cold does not cause the same problems. Pay attention to exposed skin and the temperature of the extremities to avoid tissue damage, such as frostbite.

• **Hill:** This adjusts the height of the gradient at various intervals to increase the intensity level. It allows for training to be carried out across the different training zones, i.e. low to moderate to high, and thus, depending on resistance, it ultimately works both aerobic and anaerobic systems.

• **Random:** This program keeps you guessing and can make a refreshing change. Depending on which machine you train on, it may change workloads via speed, incline, or rpm.

• **Manual:** Allows you to train at your own desired rate.

Finally, all machines have a display that gives you feedback about the quality and quantity of the exercise you are doing. If you wish, you can also wear a heart-rate monitor or take your pulse manually as you exercise to measure the intensity of the work you are doing.

using the machines

The machines that you encounter in the gym are designed to mimic the real-life action of activities such as running, rowing, and cycling, etc. For some people, running in a temperature-controlled environment where you are not at the mercy of the weather is appealing. For others, training outdoors come rain or shine has more appeal and training indoors is often the last resort. Whatever your reasons, the machines that you find in most gyms are of good quality and provide adequate scope to train all levels of exerciser. If you are not sure which machine to use, think about how you want to improve your fitness. If your aim is to feel less puffed out after running for the bus, don't spend most of your time on the bike. In other words, pick an activity or machine that is specific to your needs.

the cycle

The movement of the cycle is exactly the same as that of a normal cycle but without the need to keep oneself upright. The two common types of cycle found in the gym are the recumbent and the upright cycle. The two offer somewhat different cardiovascular effects. During recumbent cycling there is a larger stroke volume, i.e. more blood is pumped from the heart. This is because the recumbent position means that there is decreased resistance and less gravity for the heart to counteract. The recumbent cycle gives support to the back and is particularly effective for people who want to exercise soon after rehabilitation.

which muscles does it use?

- Quads
- Glutes
- Hamstrings
- Calf muscles

the treadmill

This allows you to run or walk over inclines that might not otherwise be available to you. All good treadmills come with an incline facility of 15 to 20 degrees so you can walk uphill and, on some machines, downhill.

which muscles does it use?

- Knee and hip extensors
- Quads
- Glutes
- Calf muscles

the elliptical cross trainer

The elliptical cross trainer machine (also known as an elliptical machine or a cross trainer) offers rhythmical cardiovascular exercise that is non-impact. Because cross training exercise does not involve foot strike in any phase of the movement, you will not suffer any stress on the joints that might be caused by the impact of your body weight transferring through the joints. This means that it is particularly useful for those who need to avoid high-impact exercise such as running because of knee trauma or repetitive strain injury. Since the whole body is exercised by the elliptical cross trainer, severely de-conditioned people may initially find it particularly difficult to use. However, you can set the machine to legs-only mode and, as you develop your fitness, can move on to integrating the upper body.

which muscles does it use?

Based on cross-country skiing, the elliptical cross trainer offers great cardiovascular exercise that conditions most of the major muscles in the body. It uses most of the muscles involved in flexing and extending the joints. The leg work involves predominantly the glutes and the quads. In the upper body, the chest and the backs of the upper arms are used to push the handles forward, while the muscles of the front and back of the arms are used to pull the handles back. Exercising on an elliptical cross trainer can feel a little disorientating at first and hard to co-ordinate.

the rowing machine

The rowing machine offers multi-jointed exercise that has a similar action to real life rowing. However, there is no need to take the oars from the water on each stroke! With your feet strapped into the machine at one end, the activity involves pulling on a handle that moves you along a rolling seat.

which muscles does it use?

Like the elliptical cross trainer, the rowing machine uses most of the muscles involved in flexing and extending the joints. The major muscles used during the drive phase, when the seat is forced backward, are the legs and hips, while the catch phase brings the handle into the chest and exercises the biceps, lats, and rhomboids. The return phase pulls the seat back to the start position and involves the hamstrings, but these are not subjected to the same load as is applied during the drive and catch phases. The postural muscles of the lower and mid-upper back are also used significantly on the rowing machine.

general body conditioning

Conditioning all of the major muscle groups should be the aim of any general exercise program. Those who wish to develop aerobic fitness should also incorporate a general conditioning program for the body.

The legs, hips, and trunk of the body are primarily used to stabilize and provide locomotion. The whole body is utilized during locomotion, however the following examples show exercises that can be integrated into a cardiovascular training program.

As a rule, the duration of each exercise will dictate the training response. For example, if you can only complete 8–12 repetitions (reps) of each exercise, a training adaptation will be geared toward strength development. Therefore, completing more reps over longer time periods (20 reps or more if you feel able) would be appropriate to see gains in the cardiovascular system. Remember that the load used should be significantly lower to promote these gains.

Muscular dysfunction can occur throughout the body. Postural problems often stem from the hips and back, so adequate strength and endurance in these areas is necessary in order to avoid injury. Concentrate on the exercises in this section to condition the legs, hips, and trunk. Refer to the basics of training (see pages 40-42) to see how to apply these exercises to your own program, taking into account the intensity and duration of each exercise. Attempt to carry out each exercise in a way that is specific to your conditioning needs. For example, lunging has a reasonably high correlation to movement-based activities such as running and walking. For each exercise that trains the body in a certain pattern of movement, consider doing the reverse of that movement to maintain muscular symmetry.

Muscular symmetry is often lost due to the repetitive nature of our everyday activities, jobs, and sports. Many of the body's muscles work in pairs, such as the quads and hamstrings, or biceps and triceps. If one muscle is overworked, the opposite muscle group may succumb to injury, strain, or constant pain.

Visualizing the guy ropes of a tent can help you to understand this idea. If the rope on one side of the tent is shortened and tightened, it will pull the tent out of shape to one side and weaken the opposite side. This is what can happen to your body over time if one muscle, or group of muscles, is worked or strained more than the others.

Personal trainers often work with individuals who sit in front of computers for hours. Trying to counteract this, these people may participate in exercise regimes that further exacerbate the problem, rather than address the opposing muscles that are becoming weaker. This can contribute to lower back pain, pulled muscles, and strains in normal everyday movement. Their trainers have to teach them that all the muscles need to be equally strong to counteract this and to maintain muscular symmetry. It is essential to train the muscles equally.

the lunge

Lunging conditions most of the muscles in the legs with particular emphasis on the calf, thighs, and backside muscles.

1 Stand with your legs hip-width apart, arms down by your sides. Step forward with the right leg, bending both knees to a 90-degree angle at the same time.

2 Push off to return to the start position and repeat, but this time stepping forward with the left leg. Complete 12 to 20 reps for strength endurance or, if you feel able, try more than 20 reps to assist with cardiovascular conditioning.

tip

- **If you find balancing difficult, try using a stick until it becomes a little easier.**

multi-point lunge

Lunging is an integral movement in soccer and in racquet-based sports like squash or tennis. Including the multi-point lunge in your training program will have significant benefit if you practice any of these sports.

1 Stand with your legs hip-width apart, hands either hanging loosely down by your sides or on your hips.

2 Bend the left leg and take the right leg forward at a 90-degree angle.

3 Return to the center, then repeat, taking the other leg forward.

tip

- **Hold your arms out to the side for balance if necessary.**

4 Return to the center, then bend the right leg and take the left leg straight out to the side.

5 Return to the center, then repeat, taking the right leg straight out to the side.

6 Return to the center, then repeat, bending the right leg and taking the left leg straight behind you.

7 Return to the center, then repeat, bending the left leg and taking the right leg straight behind you.

8 Once you have mastered the technique, complete 12 to 20 reps for strength endurance or try more than 20 reps to assist with cardiovascular conditioning.

variations

- Add chopping patterns as you lunge.
- Lunge while holding a barbell to add resistance.

twisties

Here the oblique muscles are used to twist the trunk or pelvis.

1 Stand with feet together and legs slightly bent.

2 Raise the arms to chest height, then jump as you twist the lower body to bring the knees and hips facing to the right and the torso facing to the left.

3 Jump again to bring the knees and hips facing to the left and the torso facing the right.

4 Continue jumping/twisting for 30 seconds and, once you have mastered the exercise, progress to 3 minutes to assist with cardiovascular conditioning.

variations

- Bend your knees to create different intensities on the thighs.

- To increase the level of resistance try working with a medicine ball held between the thighs.

hamstring kicks

Hamstrings are the thigh muscles at the rear of the leg that flex or bend the knee. They need to be conditioned to prevent them developing too much strength, resulting in tension.

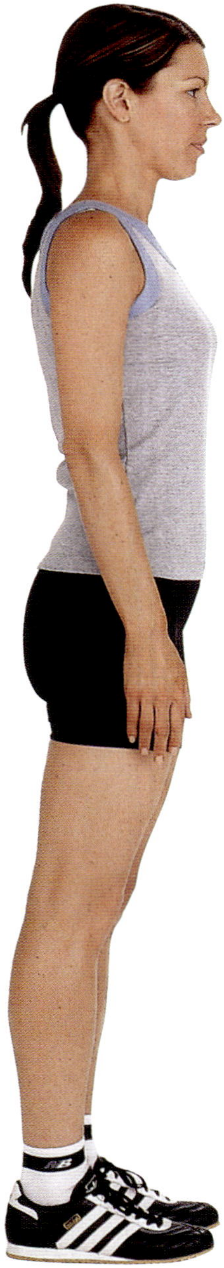

1 Stand with your feet together.

2 Then jump, bringing the heels toward the buttocks.

3 Start by jumping for 30 seconds and progress to 3 minutes.

variations

- Try holding a medicine ball between the heels as you jump.

- Hold a heavier medicine ball between the heels, releasing it as you jump.

wood chop with medicine ball

This is a multi-joint exercise that utilizes whole-body movement including a twisting of the trunk. Racquet and ball sports, such as baseball, golf, badminton, and tennis, involve a lot of twisting and rotational movements, so will improve if you include th s exercise in your program.

1 Stand with the right side of the body parallel to a wall, with the right leg straight and the left leg bent. The bent leg should bear most of the body's weight. Hold the medicine ball above your head on the left side.

2 Twist your body diagonally down toward the wall, at the same time throwing the ball so that it bounces just in front of the wall. Catch the ball and repeat.

3 Alternate sides as you repeat the exercise, doing 12 to 20 reps for strength endurance or try more than 20 to assist with cardiovascular conditioning.

tip

- You can also perform this trunk-twisting exercise using a cable station in the gym, instead of a medicine ball.

reverse chop

This exercise involves the oblique muscles to allow twisting of the trunk but it also utilizes the back muscles at the same time. These back muscles often become weak when excessive abdominal muscle exercises are done—the reverse chop allows for simultaneous abdominal and back conditioning.

1 Stand with the legs 2–3 hip-widths apart, feet parallel to each other, and holding a medicine ball in both hands.

2 Keeping the left leg straight and the feet firmly planted, bend the right leg and twist to the right to take the medicine ball just in front of the right foot.

3 Still keeping the feet planted, straighten the right leg, bend to the left, twisting the torso to raise the ball above the head.

4 Repeat to the other side. Complete 12 to 20 reps for strength endurance, alternating sides each time, or if you feel able, try completing more than 20 reps to assist with cardiovascular conditioning.

dead lift

This exercise targets the back, hamstrings, and glutes. It is often prescribed as a beginner's exercise, but it requires a good level of inter-muscular co-ordination. If you are not confident with this exercise, try one of the back exercises on pages 58, 59, and 66 as a starting point.

1 Using an overhand grip with the hands shoulder-width apart, hold a barbell in front of the body with the knees bent to about a 45-degree angle.

2 Take a deep breath and activate the deep abdominal wall by drawing the navel in toward the spine as you extend the back out of the hip to raise the bar. Slowly lower the back to the starting position. Repeat 12 to 20 times, or more depending on ability and the weight of the barbell.

tip

- To avoid injury to the lower back do not straighten the knees fully.

lateral jumps

In this exercise, the upward motion is created by the large muscles of the hips and thighs. The sideways movement is created by the internal oblique muscles of the trunk and the outer thigh muscles.

1 Imagine a line running alongside you. Lightly flex the knees and jump from side to side over the line.

variation

- You can change the height at which you jump to increase or decrease the amount of work on the thighs.

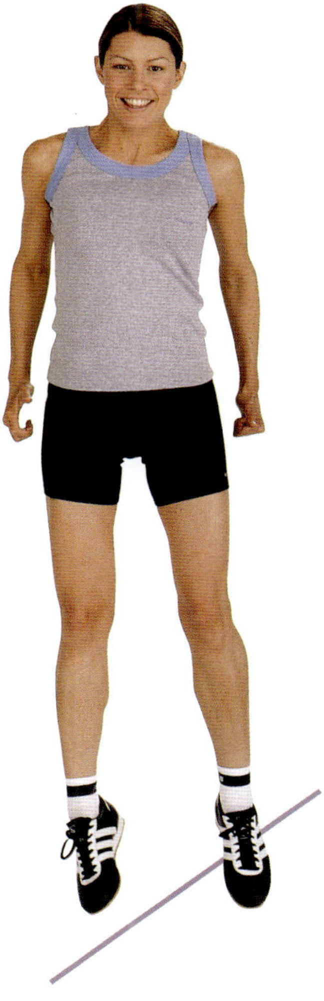

2 Start by jumping for 30 seconds and progress to 3 minutes.

step-ups

A step-up is a great functional exercise that uses all the muscles in the lower body. The postural muscles have to work to maintain good form throughout. When choosing step height, try to avoid going higher than a 90-degree angle and ensure that the knee is directly over the toes.

1 Stand facing a step and place the right foot in the middle of the step.

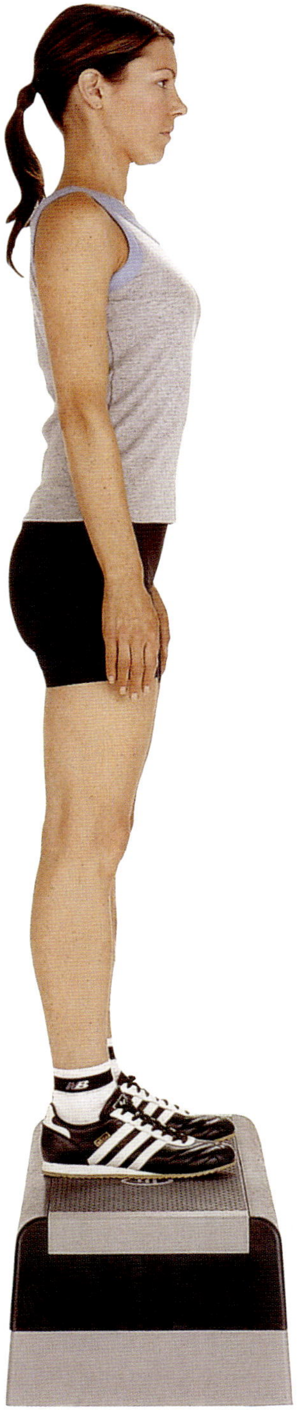

variation

- You can perform this exercise holding dumbbells in each hand for added resistance.

2 Breathe in, then breathe out as you activate the deep abdominal wall (see page 56) and take the left foot up onto the step.

3 Lower the left foot to the start position under control. Repeat, alternating legs with each step. Complete 12 to 20 reps for strength endurance or try doing more than 20 to assist with cardiovascular conditioning.

step-overs

This exercise uses the major hip and thigh muscles to push the body up and to the side. The inner and outer thigh muscles work to move the legs sideways across the step. The postural muscles, and in particular the back muscles, are working to keep the back upright.

variations

- **Jump to different points on the step to vary the stride width.**
- **Perform the same exercise on an inflatable disc to simulate a different type of terrain.**

1 Stand with the hands clenched and the left side of the body parallel with a step that is no more than 6 inches (15 cm) high. Place the left foot on the center of the step and leave the right foot on the floor and parallel to the step.

2 Jump to bring the right foot to the center of the step and then the left foot to the floor on the other side of the step.

3 Start with 30 seconds and gradually progress to 3 minutes.

ball balances

Here the muscles that are used in a lateral or sideways movements when skiing are used to move the ball underneath you. Ball balances also help to train for co-ordination and balance, which are especially useful in skiing.

1 Sit, with a straight back, on a Swiss ball.

variations

• Once you have mastered sitting on the ball, try kneeling on it and repeating the side-to-side action.

• If you can master the kneeling position and are feeling very confident, try standing on the ball. This requires good training of the core muscles.

tips

- Work on a mat—for obvious reasons!
- Even if you can only manage to balance for a couple of seconds don't give up. You'll soon make progress.

2 Move the ball from side to side by flexing the trunk.

3 Start by balancing for 30 seconds and progress to 3 minutes.

hip extensions

Hip extensions on the ball are an ideal way to start conditioning the back, glutes, and hamstrings at the same time, helping to develop inter-muscular coordination between them. This particular exercise is similar to the dead lift but without the external load provided by a barbell or dumbbell. It is a great exercise to try before the dead lift (see page 108).

1 Sit on a Swiss ball. Slowly slide your buttocks and back down the ball to lower your shoulders into position, ensuring that your head and shoulders stay centered on the ball.

2 Drop the buttocks down toward the floor keeping the hips and knees flexed.

3 Extend the hips until the trunk and hips are level then drop toward the floor. Repeat 12 to 20 times for strength endurance, progressing to more than 20 reps to assist with cardiovascular conditioning, once you have mastered the exercise.

half push-ups

Push-ups help to develop the chest, or pectoral major, and the back of the arm, or triceps. Furthermore, they also train the serratus muscles that contribute to the stability of the shoulder blades and, if carried out correctly, train the postural muscles.

1 Kneel on hands and knees on a mat on the floor, with the hands just wider than shoulder-width apart and the feet at shoulder-width. Look in a mirror or have a "spotter" or helper place a pole along the length of the spine to check that the pole makes contact with the spine in three places—at the hip, mid-back, and head.

2 Keeping the chin tucked in and facing the floor, slowly lower the body toward the floor by bending the arms outward, keeping the abdominal muscles pulled in tight and breathing in as you do so.

3 Then, while breathing out, push your body up from the floor, straighten the arms, and return to the start position. Try to complete 12 to 20 push-ups for strength endurance and,once you feel able, try to progress to more than 20 reps to assist with cardiovascular conditioning.

variation

- If you are strong enough, you can perform the full push-up with the hands and feet on the floor.

upright row

This is a multi-joint exercise that works the shoulder and elbow joints. The main muscles it uses are the biceps and those of the shoulders and upper back.

1 Use an overhand grip to hold the dumbbells in each hand in front of the body. Stand with the legs shoulder-width apart, and the knees slightly bent.

2 Breathe in and as you breathe out, take the elbows out to the side to raise the dumbbells to just below chin level.

3 Slowly lower the dumbbells back to the starting position. Repeat 12 to 20 times for strength endurance or try more than 20 reps to assist with cardiovascular conditioning.

bent-over row

This conditions the upper back muscles that are often neglected through long periods of sedentary work.

1 Using an overhand grip with the hands shoulder-width apart, hold a barbell in front of the body with the knees bent to about a 45-degree angle. Keep the spine in neutral.

2 Activate the deep abdominal wall (see page 56) to provide support for the spine. Breathe out, pulling the barbell in toward the chest, drawing the elbows behind you, and squeezing the shoulder blades together.

3 Lower the barbell in a controlled fashion, breathing in on the way down. Repeat 12 to 20 times or more depending on ability and the weight of the barbell.

squat and press

This exercise combines the squat with a shoulder press. It is a total-body exercise that uses all of the major joints—the knee, hip, elbow, and shoulder joints—and works many of the major muscles—the quads, glutes, back of shoulders, and the triceps.

1 Stand with the legs shoulder-width apart holding a medicine ball close to the chest.

2 Breathing in and gently drawing the navel inward at the same time, squat so the thighs are parallel with the floor. Keep the weight close to the chest.

3 Breathe out as you return to a standing position, pushing upward as you do so to extend the arms and raise the medicine ball above the head.

4 Lower the arms to bring the medicine ball back to chest height and return to the starting position. Complete 12 to 20 reps for strength endurance or, if you feel able, try more than 20 reps to assist with cardiovascular conditioning.

tip

- When you squat, ensure that the knee joints are not forced out beyond the toes and that the medicine ball is also held in line with the feet. Loads carried beyond the toes tend to place extra stress upon the lower back.

variations

- You can use dumbbells or barbells instead of the medicine ball.
- To further challenge the body, try throwing the ball and catching it. Ensure that a neutral spine is maintained throughout the movement.

tricep dips

This conditions the small pec muscles along with the muscles located on the rear of the upper arm.

1 Stand with the legs hip-width apart with your back toward the front edge of a chair. Take the hands behind you and, with the arms fully extended, bend the knees to slowly lower the body until you can grasp the edge of the chair seat.

2 Breathe in as you bend the arms to lower the buttocks toward the floor, ensuring that the knees stay slightly bent and keeping the buttocks close to the chair seat. Avoid rounding the back.

3 Breathe out as you push up back to the start position. Try to do 12 to 20 repetitions for strength endurance or, if you feel able, try more than 20 to assist with cardiovascular conditioning.

tip

- Do not have the feet too far forward as this causes excessive stress on the shoulders.

back extensions with ball

The back extension is probably one of the most common exercises for conditioning the back muscles. The exercise can be performed on the floor, but this version using a Swiss ball gives a better range of movement.

1 Bend the legs slightly and rest the feet against a wall while lying prone across a Swiss ball with the hands by the sides of the body. Lie with the hip joint just behind the top of the ball.

2 Raise the body until the back is fully extended. Hold for a few seconds, then lower the body back into the start position.

3 Repeat the exercise 12 to 20 times for strength endurance or try to complete more than 20 reps to assist with cardiovascular conditioning.

variations

- Hold a medicine ball as you work, tucking it into the chest as you come up.

- Change the position of the arms to add resistance, for example, cross the arms over the chest.

- Take the arms above the head.

tips

- To use the ball correctly, ensure the hip joint is positioned just behind the apex of the ball.
- Avoid going too far or hyper-extending.
- Lower down under control.

chapter 6

programs

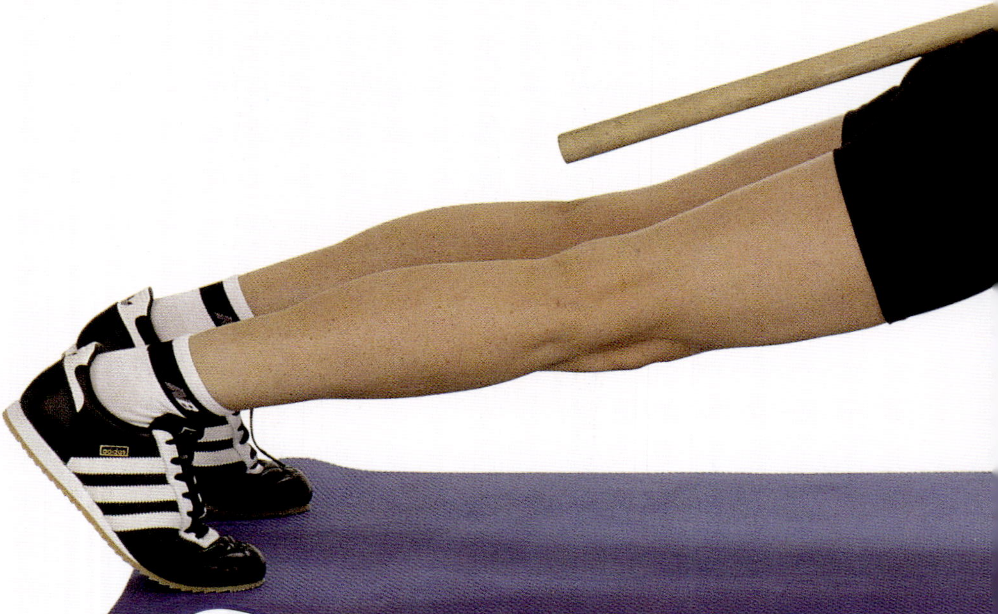

- cardiovascular exercise programs
- before you begin
- new to exercise walking program
- developing running distance program
- developing running speed program
- pregnancy training program
- post-natal training program
- ten-station circuit training program
- team sports program
- swim development program
- ski fitness program
- racquet sports program

cardiovascular exercise programs

The following programs have been specifically developed as a starting point that will set the foundation for developing your own cardiovascular exercise programs over time. They act as a kick-start to motivate you into doing regular cardiovascular activity as part of your normal healthy lifestyle and are a starting point to prepare you for achieving your first health and fitness goals.

When starting any new program, there is always a lot to learn and a lot to think about. Start slowly and carefully with the program that is most suitable for you and build from there. Do not expect too much of yourself in the beginning. It will take time for your fitness levels to improve, so don't give up if you find it difficult at first. Remember that you can't run before you can walk!

The rate of progression is indicated by volume, or amount, of training and by intensity of training. Remember that one of the laws of training is the principle of individuality. How one person might adapt to a training schedule will be totally different to another. Therefore if you find it difficult to follow one particular program, adjust the amount of training and the intensity to suit your needs. If you find a program easy, you should still attempt to follow a gradual rate of progression. This will help you to achieve your targets and, therefore, to remain motivated. It will also help to keep you injury-free.

- If you are new to exercise, start with the new to exercise walking program (page 132).
- Follow the prescribed time of exercise and intensities, unless you find the program difficult, in which case adjust to suit your needs.
- Before moving on to the developing running speed program, ensure that you fall into the criteria for vigorous exercise recommended by the ACSM (see pages 26-27).
- If you are at all unsure about your health or about how much exercise you should be doing, always seek the advice of your G.P. or a qualified fitness professional.

before you begin

The ten cardiovascular exercise programs incorporate a recommended stretch routine in addition to a week-by-week cardiovascular routine chart. The chart details the time and intensity you should maintain while performing each of the main endurance activities three to four times a week. For each of these programs, you must first complete the following warm ups and preparations before moving on to the main endurance exercise.

pre-warm up

Once you have determined that you are fit enough to begin a cardiovascular training session (see pages 26–27), you have to prepare youself for the activity you are about to do. The mobilization exercises and stretches in chapter 4 will help you to determine if you have any muscular dysfunction or restriction. Listen to your body and try the self-assessment exercises, so you can develop an understanding of your own muscles and stretching needs. If necessary, perform the appropriate corrective exercises before your warm up to stretch short tight muscles and strengthen long weak muscles.You may consider seeing a corrective exercise specialist, who can help you understand the nuances of your body, if you find it difficult to do so yourself.

warm up

Do around five minutes of light cardiovascular work similar to the main endurance component of your chosen program.

stretch program

The muscles you will be using during the main endurance exercise component need to be thoroughly stretched before you begin. These are primarily the calf, thigh, hamstring, pec minor, glutes, and hip flexor/oblique muscles. You should follow the stretch routines detailed alongside each endurance program.

main endurance component

Now you are ready to move onto your chosen main endurance component, such as walking or running. Begin by following the weekly routines detailed in each of the program charts.

cool down

When you have completed one session of your endurance exercise, be sure to finish with five minutes of light cool down exercise and streching to slowly return your blood pressure to pre-exercise levels (see page 54). Refer to the specific cool down and stretching instructions outlined in each program.

new to exercise walking program

This program is a generic cardiovascular program that is aimed primarily at the sedentary person or new exerciser. It offers a simple introduction to cardiovascular fitness through low-level walking. Before you start walking according to the intensity and time outlined in the chart below, follow the before you begin instructions (page 131) and the stretch program opposite. It is essential to warm up and stretch properly prior to any cardiovascular exercise routine.

	week 1	week 2	week 3	week 4	week 5	week 6
session 1 intensity & time	40% stamina 10 min	45% stamina 12min	50% stamina 12 min	55% stamina 15min	60% stamina 20 min	60% stamina 25 min
session 2 intensity & time	40% stamina 12 min	40% stamina 15 min	50% stamina 15 min	50% stamina 20 min	60% stamina 15 min	60% stamina 20 min
session 3 intensity & time	40% stamina 15 min	50% stamina 10 min	50% stamina 18 min	55% stamina 15 min	60% stamina 20 min	60% stamina 25 min

cool down to finish:

Do low-level cool down exercise, such as some slow walking, for 3-5 minutes.
Do the alternate superman exercise (below and page 76).
Repeat the stretch program opposite.

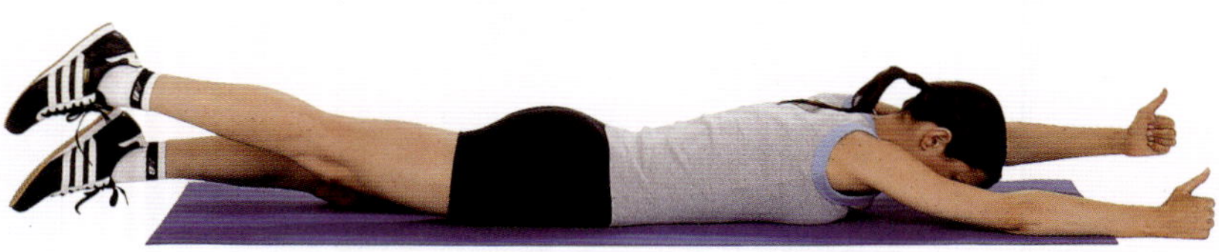

calf stretch
(see page 60)

quad and hip flexor stretch
(see page 62)

bent leg hamstring stretch
(see page 64)

pec minor stretch
(see page 71)

TFL stretch
(see page 69)

glute medius stretch
(see page 70)

developing running distance program

This program improves cardiovascular fitness by progressing to jogging. Before you start jogging according to the intensity and time outlined in the chart below, follow the before you begin instructions (page 131) and the stretch program opposite. Consider doing corrective exercises and stretches as a pre-warm up if there are muscular imbalances in your body—stretch muscles that are short and tight, not those that are long and weak. The mcKenzie press (page 75) is particularly important if your hamstrings are tight or if you have a flat lower back. A suitable warm up to prepare the body for running would be 3-5 minutes of light jogging.

	week 1	week 2	week 3	week 4	week 5	week 6
session 1 intensity & time	60% stamina 15 min	65 stamina 15min	60% stamina 20 min	65% stamina 30min	80% stamina 20 min	75% stamina 20 min
session 2 intensity & time	65% stamina 15 min	70% stamina 10 min	65% stamina 15 min	65% stamina 25 min	70% stamina 25 min	65% stamina 40 min
session 3 intensity & time	60% stamina 15 min	65% stamina 10 min	70% stamina 18 min	70% stamina 15 min	75% stamina 20 min	80% stamina 25 min
session 4 intensity & time	60% stamina 25 min	60% stamina 25 min	65% stamina 20 min	75% stamina 15 min	65% stamina 35 min	70% stamina 30 min

cool down to finish:

Do low-level cool down exercise, such as walking, for 5 minutes.
Do the prone cobra exercise (below and page 78).
Repeat the stretch program opposite.

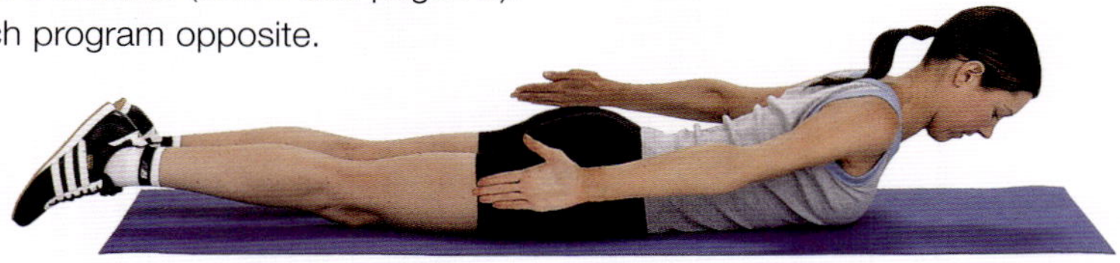

mid-upper back mobilization
(see page 59)

pec minor stretch
(see page 71)

bent leg hamstring stretch
(see page 64)

quad and hip flexor stretch
(see page 62)

TFL stretch
(see page 69)

glute medius stretch
(see page 70)

mcKenzie press
(see page 75)

developing running speed program

This program takes you on to high-intensity cardiovascular fitness by progressing to running. Before you start running according to the intensity and time outlined in the chart below, follow the before you begin instructions (page 131) and the stretch program opposite. Do not do the mcKenzie press if a kyphosis lordosis is present (see page 72). As a warm up, 5 minutes of light to moderate running will prepare the body for running at speed. Effective stretching is very important before undertaking this running speed program to ensure an adequate range of motion in all of the joints. Speed training can be quite demanding and may leave the body with DOMS (Delayed Onset Muscle Soreness) (see page 26).

	week 1	week 2	week 3	week 4	week 5	week 6
session 1 intensity & time	70% stamina 30 mins	90% stamina 3x3 mins 60 secs rest	80% stamina 25 mins	80% stamina 20 mins	95% stamina 3x2 mins 90 secs rest	75% stamina 20 mins
session 2 intensity & time	80% stamina 20 mins	85% stamina 15 mins	85% stamina 20 mins	90% stamina 5x3 mins 60 secs rest	90% stamina 4x3 mins 60 secs rest	85% stamina 15 mins
session 3 intensity & time	85% stamina 15 mins	90% stamina 4x3 mins 60 secs rest	90% stamina 5x3 mins 60 secs rest	85% stamina 15 mins	85% stamina 20 mins	95% stamina 4x2 mins 60 secs rest
session 4 intensity & time	80% stamina 20 mins	80% stamina 15-20 mins	85% stamina 15 mins	90% stamina 5x3 mins 60 secs rest	80% stamina 25 mins	70% stamina 30 mins

cool down to finish:

Do low-level cool down, such as slow jogging or walking for 5 minutes.
Do the prone cobra exercise (below and page 78).
Repeat the stretch program opposite.

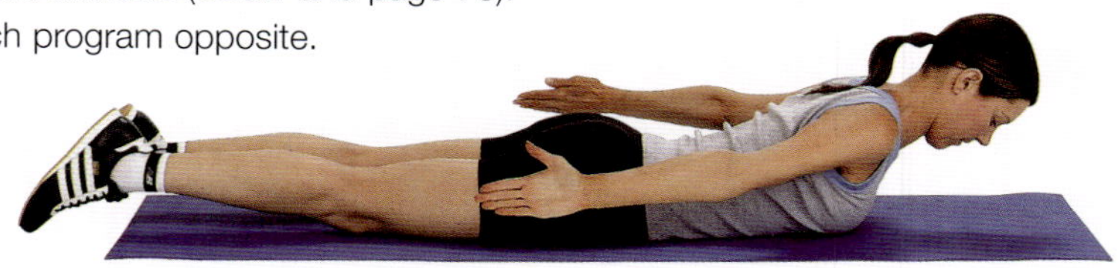

mid-upper back mobilization
(see page 59)

calf stretch
(see page 60)

standing thigh stretch
(see page 61)

quad and hip flexor stretch
(see page 62)

forward bow
(see page 63)

bent leg hamstring stretch
(see page 64)

pec minor stretch
(see page 71)

TFL stretch
(see page 69)

gluteus medius stretch
(see page 70)

mcKenzie press
(see page 75)

pregnancy training program

This program helps maintain cardiovascular fitness during pregnancy and promotes speedy recovery in the post-natal period.

There are many hypothetical risks associated with exercising, but the benefits of regular exercise during pregnancy far outweigh the risks and allow the mother to return to regular exercise soon after the birth. Exercising regularly also helps the mother to cope psychologically with the constant changes that her body is going through and may help to prevent the excessive weight gain experienced by some women. When exercising during pregnancy, take note of the following advice:

- Before you start a training program during pregnancy, always consult a doctor.

- In the past, non weight-bearing exercises such as cycling and swimming have always been recommended during pregnancy. However, walking for short periods of time is also essential and should not be ruled out.

- Exercise lying in supine (face up) positions should be avoided as this will restrict the blood flow to the uterus.

- Exercise in a well-ventilated area to avoid over-heating.

- Allow for adequate rest periods between exercises.

- Avoid excessive, high-intensity exercise as there is a decreased amount of oxygen available to the mother during pregnancy. Ideally exercise intensity should stay below 60 percent stamina.

- It is not necessary to stick to specific exercise intensities.

- Light exercise can be done throughout pregnancy. Intermittent exercise will not have the desired maintenance effect so attempt to exercise three times a week to maintain adequate levels of cardio-respiratory fitness.

- Expectant and breast-feeding women need to consume 300 to 500Kcals more per day.

- Bear in mind that a pregnant woman's functional capacity will decrease gradually over the three trimesters. This means that exercise intensity should also decrease so that exercise feels comfortable and not stressful.

- During and straight after pregnancy there are high levels of the hormone Relaxin circulating in the mother's body. This helps prepare the joints, ligaments, and tendons that are needed during delivery. For this reason, you should avoid stretching to full intensity.

You should stop exercising if:

- any bleeding occurs
- there is a rise in blood pressure or heart rate
- there is sudden swelling of the ankles
- you experience excessive fatigue
- you experience insufficient weight gain during pregnancy
- you have persistent headaches or blurred vision
- you have unexpected abdominal pains.

Before you start an exercise session as detailed in the chart below, follow the before you begin instructions (page 131) and the stretch program on the following page (page 140). During pregnancy, as at any other time, it is essential to warm up and stretch thoroughly before doing any cardiovascular exercise—and don't forget to cool down afterwards as well. The endurance component of this program includes several different cardiovascular activities that can be done in a gym, namely working on the elliptical cross trainer, the rowing machine, and the cycle, as well as general walking. Refer to the section cardiovascular training in the gym (page 90) for more information.

Many people suggest that exercise in the first trimester of pregnancy can remain at an intensity of 70 percent or so. However, the importance of intensities should always come second to staying mobile and active. As the pregnancy progresses, you should also work using a light load with less impact, and running should be replaced by walking. The times given here are only a guide. If exercise seems difficult, as little as ten minutes will be sufficient to maintain previous fitness levels.

	week 1	week 2	week 3	week 4	week 5	week 6
session 1	cycling	walking	cross trainer walking cycling	rowing walking cycling	cycling	rowing
time	20 mins	15 mins	10 mins each	10 mins each	20 mins	5-10 mins
session 2	cycling	cross trainer cycling	walking	cycling	cross trainer rowing	cycling
time	20 mins	10 mins each	20 mins	30 mins	10 mins each	10-15 mins
session 3	cross trainer	walking	cross trainer	cross trainer walking	cycling	cycling
time	15 mins	25 mins	20 mins	15 mins each	10-20 mins	10-20 mins

cool down to finish:

Follow the cardiovascular activity with pelvic floor exercises, as recommended by your doctor, midwife, or obstetrician. Repeat the stretch program on the next page.

calf stretch
(see page 60)

standing thigh stretch
(see page 61)

quad and hip flexor stretch
(see page 62)

forward bow
(see page 63)

bent leg hamstring stretch
(see page 64)

pec minor stretch
(see page 71)

TFL stretch
(see page 69)

post-natal training program

Light exercise can be resumed 6 to 8 weeks after the birth. It is important that you feel ready to exercise and are eating adequately, or you will not have high enough energy levels. This program is most suited to women who have stayed active throughout their pregnancy. If you didn't manage this, reduce the intensity of your exercise. The program is designed to give variety to someone returning to exercise. If you particularly enjoy using one piece of equipment, by all means use it, but remember the body gets used to exercising in a certain way, so keep it on its toes by giving it a new challenge from time to time. Before you start an exercise session, as detailed in the chart below, follow the before you begin instructions (page 131) and the stretch program opposite (page 140).

	week 1	week 2	week 3	week 4	week 5	week 6
session 1	treadmill	cross trainer cycling treadmill	rowing	cycling	treadmill	treadmill
intensity	40-60%	50-60%	70%	70%	60-65%	65-70%
time	10 mins	10 mins each	10-15 mins	15 mins	20 mins	15 mins
session 2	cycling	rowing	treadmill	cross trainer	cross trainer	cycling cross trainer
intensity	50-60%	40-60%	65%	70%	70%	60%
time	15 mins	5-10 mins	15-20 mins	10 mins	12-15 mins	10 mins each
session 3	cross trainer	cycling	cycling	treadmill	rowing cross trainer treadmill	cross trainer treadmill
intensity	40-60%	60%	65%	70%	60%	65-70%
time	10 mins	25 mins	20 mins	10-15 mins	10 mins each	12 mins each

cool down to finish:

The four-point prone exercise (right and page 79).
Follow with either the full superman (page 77) or the prone cobra (page 78).
Do low-level cool down for 5 minutes.
Repeat the stretch program opposite.

ten-station circuit training program

Circuit training has been a cornerstone of fitness and athletic training for thousands of years. It involves the use of a sequence of exercises carried out on a range of equipment that, ideally, works a number of the larger muscle groups. This ten-station circuit program is designed to elicit a cardiovascular training response by continually keeping the heart in the desired training zone. Prior to starting this exercise program, refer to the before you begin instructions (page 131) and ensure you always warm up and cool down effectively with a few minutes of light cardiovascular work and suitable stretches.

Many people who are in a de-conditioned state go to a circuit class and are encouraged to exercise beyond their capacity. This will encourage a "form break" or inability to complete the exercise properly. Always work at your own capacity during circuit training. If you can't do an exercise well, don't do it! Try to deconstruct the exercise and break into its individual parts, become skilled at it, then attack it with vigor. The Ten-station circuit training program here is just one example of thousands of different types of circuits. They can be conducted in a class or on a selection of fixed stations. If you only have fixed-weight resistance machinery available to you, always remember to include appropriate core-conditioning exercises at the end of the session. Examples of these can be found on pages 96-127.

For the best cardiovascular training, bear in mind the following points:

- In order to maintain the emphasis on cardiovascular development, you should work at levels less than 90 percent of your maximum heart rate (see pages 32-35).

- If you get to the point where you cannot physically talk, you should consider taking a rest as you are starting to work the anaerobic pathway. This will stress other energy systems and may affect your cardiovascular development.

- The amount of time spent on each circuit can be manipulated to increase cardiovascular capacity, muscular strength, and endurance.

- The weight or resistance selected should allow for at least 30 to 60 seconds of work at each station. Each repetition should be completed with good form.

- After completing each station of the circuit rest for no more than one minute to promote a cardiovascular training effect.

- As you work, especially when using heavier loads, you should be sure to draw the deep abdominal wall in toward the spine, to prevent any injuries.

- Breathe in as you lift, and out after the hardest part of the lift (the "sticking point") while still attempting to draw the navel in.

wood chop
(see page 104)

half push-ups
(see page 118)

multi-point lunge
(see page 98)

hip flexor and oblique stretch
(see page 65)

upright row
(see page 120)

tricep dips
(see page 124)

squat and press
(see page 122)

hip extensions
(see page 116)

bent-over row
(see page 121)

step-ups
(see page 110)

team sports program

Team sports are a great way of staying healthy and fit. In most sporting calendars there is a competitive period then a layoff or rest period before the next competitive season. However, pre-season training is often inadequate to prepare the weekend warrior for the season ahead.

For this reason you should ensure that cardiovascular training plays a major role during the initial conditioning phase before you start specific conditioning and sports-specific exercise. This initial conditioning will allow the cardiovascular system to develop general levels of aerobic fitness so you can gradually increase the intensity of your exercise. This helps to avoid injuries. You will also have more confidence and be better motivated if you follow a structured, gradual progression.

The program detailed in the chart below is designed to take a sports person from a moderate level of fitness to an increased level of fitness over a pre-season 6-week period.

Prior to starting an exercise session, refer to the Before you begin instructions (page 131) and ensure you always warm up and cool down effectively with a few minutes of light cardiovascular work and suitable stretches.

	monday	**tuesday**	**wednesday**	**thursday**	**friday**	**saturday**	**sunday**
week 1	jogging	circuit training	light jog	day off	run	circuit training	day off
week 2	intervals	light run	day off	circuit training	light run	day off	run 70–80% stamina
week 3	circuit training	run	day off	fartlek run	light run	day off	day off
week 4	specific sprints	run	day off	intervals	moderate run & skills	day off	run
week 5	specific sprints	day off	interval & skills	light 20 mins aerobic	day off	friendly game	day off
week 6	sprints & skills	fartlek run	day off	moderate run 70% 20–30 mins	day off	first competitive game	day off

swim development program

The program detailed in the chart below is designed to help the non-swimmer progress from pool walking to swimming. It is important to take this program at your own pace, moving on to the next stage as and when you feel comfortable, rather than on a strict daily or weekly basis.

Try to use the training variables of heart rate and RPE to evaluate your progress. If you feel that your swimming doesn't progress well, try doing poolside drills such as kicks to develop leg technique and help you to improve your confidence in the water.

Prior to starting any of the exercise sessions detailed below, refer to the Before you begin instructions (page 131) and ensure you always warm up and cool down effectively with a few minutes of light cardiovascular work and suitable stretches.

session 1	Stand with water at hip to chest level and progress from pool walking to jogging to elevate your heart rate to the appropriate training zone (see HRR calculation pages 36-37). Try a 5 to 10 minute session.
session 2	With the water at chest level, increase the time spent walking or jogging to 10 to 20 minutes.
session 3	Attempt to complete three 10-minute bursts of running or walking at the appropriate heart-rate training zone.
session 4	Attempt to swim as many widths or lengths as you can while maintaining your appropriate heart-rate training zone. If you only manage a minute or two, use the rest of the 30 minutes to walk or jog across the pool.
session 5	Attempt to swim for 15 minutes, using the remaining 15 minutes to walk or jog across the pool.
session 6	Attempt to swim for 15 to 30 minutes while maintaining your appropriate heart-rate training zone.

ski fitness program

Christmas comes but once a year and so does the snow and for many skiers this is the most exercise they will do all year round. Yet even recreational skiing is a demanding activity that involves cardiovascular, strength and co-ordination training. People who go skiing without having raised their base levels of fitness may be asking for a nasty injury. Most people don't grasp the concept that if they took a little time to raise their fitness levels they would get a lot more out of their skiing.

Skiing is an activity that uses many different joints but the emphasis is on the trunk and lower limbs. The obliques are used to decelerate the pelvis after twisting and turning and the thigh muscles need to be able to constantly bend and straighten as they react to the undulating terrain.

When you start this circuit, do each exercise for just 30 seconds followed by simply walking for approximately 30 seconds as a rest. The whole circuit should last approximately 5 minutes. As you slowly progress to doing each exercise for 3 minutes, the entire circuit will take 17 to 19 minutes and will ensure that the legs and postural muscles are subjected to a progressive cardiovascular overload. Ensure that your active walking lasts less than 60 seconds in order to overload the slow twitch (type I) muscle fibers.

Once you have completed this ski fitness program, if you feel that you are capable of more, you can add some additional cardiovascular training in the form of running, walking, or using the elliptical cross trainer for around 10 to 20 minutes.

Refer to the before you begin instructions (page 131) prior to starting this circuit and don't forget to warm up and cool down effectively with a few minutes of light cardiovascular work and suitable stretches.

safety tips for skiing

- Always wear a good sun block and shades. The reflective glare off snow can leave you with bad burns and damaged sight if you're not careful.

- Drink lots of water. Your surroundings may be cold but you'll sweat a lot with the exertion of exercise and you need to keep hydrated.

- Stretching your limbs after a skiing session can make a big difference to how stiff you feel the next day!

- Don't be too ambitious. If you're a novice, don't aim for slopes that are beyond your capabilities. You'll be nervous, your muscles will tense, and if you fall you will land badly.

lateral jumps
(see page 109)

walking for 30 seconds
(see page 85)

twisties
(see page 100)

walking for 30 seconds
(see page 85)

hamstring kicks
(see page 102)

walking for 30 to 60 seconds
(see page 85)

ball balances
(see page 114)

walking for 30 to 60 seconds
(see page 85)

step-overs
(see page 112)

racquet sports program

Racquet sports such as tennis, badminton, and squash demand that players are capable of running, twisting, bending, and extending for prolonged periods of time. An effective shot can earn a point in seconds but a rally can last several minutes so in the course of a game the player's body alternates between short-term and aerobic energy systems.

Without appropriate conditioning players leave themselves open to possible injury. Most will benefit from cardiovascular conditioning to provide a base level of fitness before they progress to sports-specific conditioning.

If you play racquet sports, try combining cardiovascular conditioning with the strength and endurance circuit opposite that targets the specific muscles you use. Also consider which muscles might become weak due to the dominance of one side. In addition to providing pre-game training this circuit can help to improve and maintain performance. The exercises can be included in a training program once a base level of cardiovascular conditioning has been achieved. Remember the guidelines on pages 40–42 to help you achieve your desired gains.

Refer to the before you begin instructions (page 131) prior to exercising and warm up and cool down effectively with a few minutes of cardiovascular work and suitable stretches.

	monday	tuesday	wednesday	thursday	friday	saturday	sunday
week 1	run 60–70%	racquet circuit	day off	run	day off	game	day off
week 2	racquet circuit	run	postural work	day off	light run	game	day off
week 3	intervals 85–90%	light run 30–40 mins 65–70%	circuits 45–60 mins	light run 15 mins	day off	game	day off
week 4	racquet circuit 30–45 mins	day off	intervals 90%	day off	light run	game	day off
week 5	fartlek run	racquet circuit	light run 20 mins 70%	day off	day off	game	day off
week 6	racquet circuit 30–45 mins	light run 20–30 mins 70%	racquet circuit 45–60 mins	light run 20–30 mins 70%	day off	game	day off

multi-point lunge
(see page 98)

multi-point lunge variation
(see page 99)

dead lift
(see page 108)

wood chop with medicine ball
(see page104)

hamstring kicks
(see page 102)

reverse chop
(see page 106)

twisties
(see page 100)

twisties variation
(see page 101)

back extensions with ball
(see page 126)

back extensions with ball variation
(see page 127)

chapter 7

final thoughts

- top tips for successful lifelong exercise
- training myths exploded
- assessment tools
- special advice for diabetics

top tips for successful lifelong exercise

Remember that the commitment to exercise should be adopted as a lifelong strategy by anyone who wants a longer, healthier life. Exercising for health can be conducted at fairly light intensities. Some people are happy to plod on at this pace, while others may find this tedious after a while and may want to do exercises that are more complex and demanding and which require higher levels of commitment. Whatever your needs and goals, the following tips will help to keep you on track.

- Variety is the key to staying motivated, so try new exercises on a regular basis.

- Remember to alternate volume and intensity throughout your training schedule.

- Always stay well hydrated while doing any cardiovascular training.

- Staying in the gym for extended periods of time is a waste of your efforts: quality not quantity should be your aim.

- Record your progress.

- Analyze your efforts and think about where you can make improvements.

- If you are working in a gym, avoid copying the person on the next machine just because it looks good. Stick to your own program.

- Training for strength and training for endurance should be completed on separate days.

- Eat for performance: change any bad dietary habits and see what a difference it makes to your energy levels.

- Wear appropriate clothing according to the environment you are working in.

- If you ever have to stop training for more than a week, when you return, decrease your training intensity and work back up.

- Taking half an hour each month to reassess and plan your training schedule will help you to focus better and develop your goals and strategies. A suitable schedule may even save you time in the long run. Plan for success.

- Training for more than an hour can have negative effects on your progression and may contribute to over-training syndrome (see page 41). Instead, aim to complete 30–60 minutes at least five times a week—after all, half an hour out of the day is not so unrealistic for most people.

training myths exploded

There are many old wives' tales that I have heard during my time on the gym floor. If you ever hear one of these "pearls of wisdom," you will know why it should be ignored.

• **Training while wearing lots of clothes or even black bin liners will help you lose weight:** True, you will lose weight, but most of it will be some of the 60 percent water that your body weight consists of and it will return as soon as you have replaced the body's fluids. The body needs this water, so exercising in this way is dangerous as it can lead to dehydration and restrict your ability to exercise correctly.

• **Exercise to sweat out a cold:** When you are ill the body requires a lot of energy to fight the infection, so do yourself a favor, take a day off, give yourself some TLC and return to training a lot quicker.

• **Train to get rid of a hangover:** Excessive alcohol in your system is like having diesel in a petrol engine: the body has to work overtime to expel the toxins. Instead, drink lots of fluids (non alcoholic!) to help flush out the system.

• **No pain no gain:** It's time we all got away from these old ideas. Yes, exercise for performance does require determination and perseverance but health-related gains can be achieved at significantly lower levels of exercise intensity. Trying to train through the pain simply increases the level of physical pain you feel. Pain is the body's way of telling us it is not functioning properly—listen to it.

• **Women can develop large muscles through weight training:** The hormone oestrogen ensures that women find it inherently difficult to develop large muscles, even through resistance training. In fact, I advocate that women participate in weight training combined with a cardiovascular training program—albeit on separate days.

• **Stitches are the result of too much food:** The real reason why people get stitches is unclear. Remember that some people get stitches in their ribs and shoulder areas, not just the stomach. Research indicates that it could be caused by gaseous exchange at a cellular level, but this has not been proven. It is prudent, however, not to eat for at least 45 minutes before exercising.

• **You don't start burning fat until after 20 minutes of cardiovascular exercise:** Wrong. We are constantly breathing in order to supply oxygen to the working muscles, albeit at a low level, therefore, fat is being used as a fuel even when we are asleep.

• **You shouldn't drink water during exercise:** The number of people you see who go through their whole exercise routine without drinking is unbelievable. Remember that drinking water is second only to breathing air.

assessment tools

Many exercise participants train with no regard for the quality of the effort that they are putting in. I've even seen people reading a magazine while running on the treadmill!

If you are unable to assess the quality of your training, your chances of progress are slim, so record your progress in a training diary. This will help you keep track of how you are doing and will provide valuable information if you want to design a new program for yourself.

Here's an example of an exercise log to evaluate performance and provide feedback.

days	mode	distance	intensity	heart rate	time	RPE	comments
monday							
tuesday							
wednesday							
thursday							
friday							
saturday							
sunday							

special advice for diabetics

Diabetes is a metabolic disease that affects the amount of insulin—the hormone responsible for the regulation of blood glucose levels—that can be produced by the body. If left unchecked, diabetes can cause hyperglycemia or high blood-sugar levels.

There are two types of diabetes: Type I and Type II. Type I is insu in-dependant and sufferers usually require a daily injection of insulin. Type II can be controlled by medication or, in early cases, by regular cardiovascular exercise and dietary modifications.

Exercise has a similar effect on the body to insulin and can often cause hypoglycemia or low blood-sugar levels. This can also occur if too much insulin has been taken. The ACSM recommends the following guidelines for diabetics who wish to exercise:

- Measure blood glucose levels before, during, and after exercise.
- Avoid exercise when insulin levels are high.
- Unplanned exercise should be preceded by extra carbohydrates.
- If exercise is planned, insulin must be decreased before and after.
- During exercise readily available carbohydrates may need to be eaten.
- Exercisers should be aware of the signs and symptoms of hypo/hyperglycemia.
- Try to exercise with a partner.

If you are a diabetic who has never exercised before, you should have an examination by your G.P. before starting any exercise program. If you wish to design your own cardiovascular training program, you should ideally follow the guidelines for developing cardio respiratory fitness suggested earlier. You should also note the following points:

- Stamina or V02 max should be initiated at a rate of 40–50 percent.
- There is no need to progress to higher intensities; working at 50 percent will have similar effects as higher intensities.
- Ideal exercise times should increase from 20 to 60 minutes.
- If 20 minutes feels too much, aim for at least 10 minutes of continuous exercise.
- ACSM recommendations are for at least 30 minutes on all or most days.
- If you are suffer from obesity, a weight-loss program should be part of your regime. This will help to reduce the diabetic effect and may allow for reduced medication or control by exercise and diet alone.

resources

books

Guidelines for Exercise Testing and Prescription
Lippincott, Wilkins, and Williams
American College of Sports Medicine (2000)

Periodization: The Theory and Methodology of Training
T. Bompa
Champaign, IL Human Kinetics (1999)

The Psychological Basis of Physical Exertion
G.A.V. Borg
Medicine and Science in Sports and Exercise, 14 (5), pp. 377–381 (1982)

Eat Move and Be Healthy
P. Chek
C.H.E.K. Institute. San Diego, CA. (2004)

Scientific Back Conditioning
P. Chek
C.H.E.K. Institute. San Diego, CA. (2002)

Manual of Nutrition
HMSO
The Stationery Office (1999)

Health and Fitness Instructors' Handbook
Howley and Franks
Champaign, IL Human Kinetics (1997)

Concurrent Strength and Endurance Training
M. Leveritt, P.J. Abernethy, B.K. Barry, and P.A. Logan
Sports Medicine, (6) pp. 413–427 (1999)

Essentials of Exercise Physiology
McArdle, Katch, and Katch
Champaign, IL Human Kinetics (2000)

Habitual Exercise and the Age-Associated Decline in Large Artery Compliance
D.R. Seals
Exercise and Sport Science Reviews, (2) pp. 68–72 (2003)

useful Web sites

www.acsm.org
Considered the leading organization in sports medicine research for the fitness industry.

www.association-of-womens-fitness.org
Useful advice about women's fitness.

www.bhfactive.org.uk
The British Heart Foundation Web site has advice on exercise, nutrition, and living a healthy lifestyle.

www.chekinstitute.com
A groundbreaking organization that specializes in corrective and performance exercise for both athletes and non-athletes.

www.gssiweb.org
The Gatorade Sports Science Institute Web site is appealing to all levels of visitor.

www.nutrition.org.uk
The British Nutrition Foundation is a very good source of extensive nutritional information.

www.peakfitnessgroup.co.uk
The author's personal training organization, which provides a high level of sport and exercise consultancy.

www.personalhealthzone.com
Articles and links on health, fitness, weight loss, and nutrition.

www.postnatalexercise.co.uk
Specialized exercise courses for mothers during the childbearing years.

www.prevention.com
Health and fitness site with a versatile content.

www.sportsinjurybulletin.com
Tips to help avoid sports injury and radically improve overall athletic performance.

www.wholefitness.com
This Web site includes simple stretching suggestions for warming-up and cooling-down.

index

Entries in *italics* refer to stretches or exercises